GEORGINA FUGGLE is a chef and food stylist who has trained at Leith's, worked for Green & Black's and been a Senior Food Editor. She grew up helping her father with his vegetable patch and now runs several pop-up restaurants called Hart & Fuggle, with her friend Alice Hart. She is the author of *Take One Pot* and *Take One Veg*. Her blog is **fuggleantics.blogspot.com**

✳

SUPER-EASY,
NOURISHING RECIPES FOR
LENTILS, BEANS & PEAS

✳

GEORGINA FUGGLE

PHOTOGRAPHY BY ALI ALLEN

KYLE BOOKS

First published in Great Britain in 2017
by Kyle Books, an imprint of Kyle Cathie Ltd
192-198 Vauxhall Bridge Road
London SW1V 1DX
general.enquiries@kylebooks.com
www.kylebooks.co.uk

10 9 8 7 6 5 4 3 2 1

ISBN 978 0 85783 362 4

Designer **Helen Bratby**
Photographer **Ali Allen**
Food Stylist **Georgina Fuggle**
Props Stylst **Ali Allen**
Project Editor **Sophie Allen**
Copy Editor **Stephanie Evans**
Editorial Assistant **Hannah Coughlin**
Production **Nic Jones,
Gemma John** and **Lisa Pinnell**

A Cataloguing in Publication
record for this title is available
from the British Library.

Colour reproduction: ALTA London
Printed in China by 1010 Printing
International Ltd.

an introduction to perfect pulses

For the last year, chickpeas have replaced my chicken, and pinto beans my pasta, such is their impact on both me and my family's diet. Miniature dried pulses seem to appear around our home with unexplainable concentration, a skill known only before with complimentary biros. Their impact has wholeheartedly been a welcome change and has changed the way we eat, little by little, bean by bean.

Pulses are delicious. For generations, pulses have been the mainstay of the family menu, frequently appearing in our household favourites like hot chilli con carne, wholesome hummus or homemade soups, but just recently, this superfood has been battling for use in other (less familiar) recipes – cakes, breads and flours. The recipes within this book reflect the full spectrum, from traditional to experimental.

Pulses are vivacious. When you wonder past the 'pulse section' either in a dusty market in Mysore or a strip-lit supermarket in Manchester you are hit by the wealth of colour! As an ingredient, this is a huge bonus as when we eat we use all our senses; not just taste, but also smell, sight and touch/texture. The beautiful shades of pulses do not only please our eyes but help to delight our tastebuds. It was, therefore, an obvious way to divide this book. Indulge yourselves in the chapters that follow, separated by colour. It struck me that many cooks might know of a 'white bean' but may not feel quite confident enough to name the variety and I hope this colour distinction will help you navigate the plethora of pulses. White, black, green, yellow, red and brown cover all the bases and will act as your colour palette. Each bean will have its own story; the haricot, for example, is most familiar to us as the classic baked bean but is equally perfect when paired with slow-cooked lamb. A newfound favourite is the buttery French flageolet, picked before full maturity and dried in the shade to retain its distinctive green glaze – stunning when thrown into a salad or whizzed with garlic, lemon and ricotta for a simple dip.

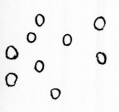

Pulses are pleasing. I'm not ashamed to say that tins of cooked pulses have become my preference and as such you will notice many recipes include these. They suit my lifestyle, with a family that often require rapid feeding.

Pulses are nutritious. Each one is essentially a little seed and each seed is a little package so powerful that an entire plant can sprout and grow. It is no wonder, then, that they are a rich source of complex carbohydrate and protein. As if that wasn't enough, they are also stuffed with fibre (far more than brown rice), folate (considerably more than kale) and loaded with antioxidants. With pulses it is not just about what they are have but also what they do not have – let us not forget that they are entirely gluten- and fat-free.

Pulses (sometimes) need preparation. Dried pulses usually need soaking (see pages 8–10) and lentils should always be rinsed. I've learned along the way to wash tinned beans thoroughly but gently, removing any claggy brine. Too much haste or force might reduce the contents to slush. In nearly all cases, the tinned beans should be added at the end of the cooking time so as not to cook any further. Though tinned beans are quicker and easier to use, the dried varieties offer far more scope for control within a recipe. With soaked, dried beans you are able to gently layer up flavour and stop cooking when the texture is perfect. A word of warning: the age of the bean when picked can dramatically affect its cooking time, so be conscious of this and feel confident to reduce or increase simmering stages as needed. Dried beans are also a more cost-effective option and make feeding a crowd on a budget, totally possible. A well-spiced dhal, lovingly cooked over the course of an afternoon, topped with crispy onions, a dollop of sour yogurt and fresh roti is one of my favourite suppers and costs very little.

So it's time to get excited, get cooking and get eating as you put your hands on the pulse.

a colour pallette of pulses

Discover the pulse palette, divided here by colour as this seems as healthy a distinction. Of course, there are many more, but this selection includes my favourites, each having a well established place in my pantry.

BROAD BEANS   RUNNER BEANS   PEAS

FLAGEOLET BEANS   GREEN SPLIT PEAS   GREEN LENTILS   EDAMAME BEANS   MUNG BEANS

YELLOW SPLIT PEAS   SPLIT FAVA BEANS   CHICKPEAS   SOYA BEANS

BLACK-EYED BEANS

PUY LENTILS

BLACK BELUGA LENTILS

BLACK BEANS

RED SPLIT LENTILS

KIDNEY BEANS

ADUKI BEANS

TINNED BORLOTTI BEANS

PINTO BEANS

BORLOTTI BEANS

BUTTER BEANS

CANNELLINI BEANS

GIGANTE BEANS

HARICOT BEANS

about the different pulses

ADUKI BEANS
Aduki beans are the tiny red beans popular in China and Japan that taste similar to a kidney bean. They are often made into a paste and stuffed into sweet, sticky rice in Asian desserts. The beans are high in protein, iron and folate, and now readily available, cooked or uncooked.
DO THEY NEED SOAKING? YES
COOKING FROM SOAKED 40
MINUTES AT A SIMMER
BUY DRIED OR TINNED

BLACK-EYED BEANS/PEAS
These are pale in colour with a distinctive black dot. They come from the cow pea family, have a distinctive starchy texture and are packed with protein while being seriously low in calories.
DO THEY NEED SOAKING? OPTIONAL
COOKING FROM SOAKED 20–30
MINUTES AT A SIMMER
COOKING FROM UNSOAKED 45
MINUTES AT A SIMMER
BUY DRIED OR TINNED

BLACK BEANS
Also known as turtle beans because of their hard shell-like appearance, these are thought to be great for aiding digestion. They are full of protein, thiamin and magnesium. Be warned that when cooking the liquid will turn a smoky-purpleish colour. Often used in sweet cooking as they develop a slightly sweet note, reminiscent of chocolate.

DO THEY NEED SOAKING? YES
COOKING FROM SOAKED 1½–2
HOURS AT A SIMMER
BUY DRIED OR TINNED

BLACK BELUGA LENTILS
These beauties glisten when they're cooked, which makes them look like beluga caviar. They are amazing in soups and look visually striking in salads.
DO THEY NEED SOAKING? NO
COOKING 20–30 MINUTES AT
A SIMMER
BUY DRIED OR TINNED

BORLOTTI BEANS
These are a type of kidney bean and, once cooked, are a light brown mottled colour, reminiscent of an Italian masterpiece and often used in Italian cooking. The fresh beans, although sometimes tricky to get hold of, are stunning when raw. They dull on cooking, but still have a gorgeous nutty taste.
DO THEY NEED SOAKING? DRIED
BEANS – YES. FRESH BEANS – NO
COOKING FROM SOAKED 1¼–1½
HOURS AT A SIMMER
BUY FRESH. DRIED OR TINNED

BROAD BEANS
My dad's favourite garden vegetable, so a familiar one for me growing up! Hearty, slightly bitter beans when eaten complete with their skins, but they're much nicer and prettier double-podded

to reveal the bright green jewels inside. Slit each pod along its seam and run your thumb along the furry inside to push the beans out.
DO THEY NEED SOAKING? NO
COOKING 4–5 MINUTES IN BOILING
WATER
BUY FRESH

BUTTER BEANS
These are large, flat, yellow-white beans, with a creamy texture and are relatively 'in vogue'. They are high in fibre, protein and low in fat, and make a killer purée.
DO THEY NEED SOAKING? YES
COOKING FROM SOAKED 1.5–2
HOURS AT A SIMMER
BUY DRIED OR TINNED

CANNELLINI BEANS
My personal favourite. Also known as white kidney beans, they are from the haricot bean family. These off-white beans are long and oval and have a soft, buttery texture. Delicious, inexpensive and easy to get hold of!
DO THEY NEED SOAKING? YES
COOKING FROM SOAKED A HARD
BOIL FOR 10 MINUTES, THEN A
FURTHER 1.5–2 HOURS
BUY DRIED OR TINNED

CHICKPEAS
These yellow, medium-sized round peas hold their shape really well when cooked. They have a gorgeous, nutty flavour and are

delicious added to soups and curries, but are famously used for making protein-rich hummus.
DO THEY NEED SOAKING? YES
COOKING FROM SOAKED 2–3 HOURS AT A SIMMER
BUY DRIED OR TINNED

....

EDAMAME BEANS

These are young soya beans, often presented still in their pods and eaten as a sweet, fresh protein-filled snack. For ease, frozen pre-podded, bright green beans are available in many supermarkets or health-food shops. These are the version I tend to cook with.
DO THEY NEED SOAKING? NO
COOKING 5–6 MINUTES AT A SIMMER
BUY FROZEN

....

FLAGEOLET BEANS

Small, creamy, pale green beans with a tender skin and sweet, creamy flavour, these are much prized in France. They are actually small, young haricot beans that have been harvested and dried in the shade to retain their green colour. Use them in salads, dips or fresh spring stews.
DO THEY NEED SOAKING? YES
COOKING 1¾–2¼ HOURS AT A SIMMER
BUY DRIED OR TINNED

....

GIGANTE BEANS

Huge, starchy, plump, gorgeous things that really look like bloated butter beans. They are loved in Greece and Spain, where they are often used in salads and stews.
DO THEY NEED SOAKING? YES
COOKING FROM SOAKED 1¼–1½ HOURS AT A SIMMER
BUY DRIED OR TINNED/JARRED

....

GREEN LENTILS

These are the standard khaki-coloured, fibre-rich lentils you see on supermarket shelves everywhere. They tend to go mushy if overcooked, so if you want them firm, add oil to the cooking water and cook the lentils only briefly.
DO THEY NEED SOAKING? NO
COOKING 30 MINUTES AT A SIMMER
BUY DRIED OR TINNED

....

GREEN PEAS

Fresh peas are at their best when shelled from the plump pods and eaten within hours of cooking. However, their season is short, so opt for the frozen variety, which in my opinion are delicious, easy to source and still retain the distinctive sweetness of fresh peas.
DO THEY NEED SOAKING? NO
COOKING 5 MINUTES IN BOILING WATER
BUY FROZEN OR FRESH

....

GREEN SPLIT PEAS

Green split peas are halved dried green peas. They are full of protein and have a lovely mild sweetness. They cook quite quickly so the trick is to catch them just before they lose their shape. They are best known for the infamous pea and ham soup.
DO THEY NEED SOAKING? NO
COOKING 30–40 MINUTES AT A SIMMER
BUY DRIED

....

HARICOT BEANS

These small, off-white oval beans cook to a fluffy, creamy consistency inside. They are most famously dressed up in tomato sauce and served as 'baked beans'. They are known for being good at absorbing the flavour of a dish.
DO THEY NEED SOAKING? YES
COOKING FROM SOAKED 1½–2 HOURS AT A SIMMER
BUY DRIED OR TINNED

....

KIDNEY BEANS

These are long, curved red beans that are high in fibre, iron and magnesium. They release carbohydrates slowly, making them a great source of energy, so it is worth adding a can to soups and stews. Dried kidney beans contain a natural toxin called lectin, which can cause stomach aches., but the toxin is destroyed by proper cooking
DO THEY NEED SOAKING? YES
COOKING FROM SOAKED BOIL FOR 10 MINUTES. THEN COOK SLOWLY FOR 1½–2 HOURS
BUY DRIED OR TINNED

MUNG BEANS

These are beautiful, small greeny-yellow beans with a tiny white stripe along their seam. They can be cooked into curries and soups, or sprouted (like bean sprouts). Stacked with protein and low in calories – boom!

DO THEY NEED SOAKING? **OPTIONAL**
COOKING FROM SOAKED **40 MINUTES AT A SIMMER**
COOKING FROM DRIED **1¼ HOURS AT A SIMMER**
BUY DRIED

PINTO BEANS

These are buff, pinky beans that become a mottled, deep brown rusty colour when cooked. Famous for filling burritos and eating, slowly cooked, with rice. Or the Mexicans love these refried and served for breakfast for an early hit of fibre and folate.

DO THEY NEED SOAKING? **YES**
COOKING FROM SOAKED **1½–2¼ HOURS AT A SIMMER**
BUY DRIED OR TINNED

PUY LENTILS

The beautiful ones: dark black and elegant. Puy lentils have a very mild peppery and slightly meaty flavour, and remain quite firm once cooked. As the name suggests, they are often used in French recipes. It's worth noting that they are also great for sprouting and amazing for your body, being a good source of iron, protein and dietary fibre.

DO THEY NEED SOAKING? **NO**
COOKING **20–30 MINUTES AT A SIMMER**
BUY DRIED OR TINNED

RED SPLIT LENTILS

High in folate and fibre, these well-known lentils have a mild, often earthy, flavour and are best if cooked with assertive flavourings. Be cautious not to overcook as they have a tendency to turn to mush.

DO THEY NEED SOAKING? **NO**
COOKING **15–20 MINUTES AT A SIMMER**
BUY DRIED

RUNNER BEANS

Runner beans are a popular garden vegetable that should be eaten whole with no need to pod. The green flesh is fresh, crunchy and slightly sweet. Be warned, pick the beans before they turn too old to avoid an unpleasant stringy texture.

DO THEY NEED SOAKING? **NO**
COOKING **5–6 MINUTES IN BOILING WATER**
BUY FRESH

SOYA BEANS

These yellow, round beans have been eaten in the Far East for thousands of years (famously, they are the base to the fermented miso soup) before making their way to the West. Here, given their high-protein levels, they are used for a multitude of meat-substitute products, such as tofu. When not transformed into other uses, the beans can simply be cooked and used in salads or soups. Soya beans contain a natural toxin called a trypsin inhibitor, which can stop you digesting food properly. This toxin is destroyed by proper cooking, so treat them carefully.

DO THEY NEED SOAKING? **YES**
COOKING **45–60 MINUTES IN BOILING WATER**
BUY DRIED OR TINNED

SPLIT FAVA BEANS

It turns out that fava beans (a variety of broad bean) are having a renaissance. They are an important part of a crop rotation system, so farmers have carried on growing them, and now, consumers have decided they taste very good. They are often mashed as they make a buttery, smooth, protein rich purée.

DO THEY NEED SOAKING? **NO (IF SPLIT)**
COOKING **40 MINUTES AT A SIMMER**
BUY DRIED OR TINNED

YELLOW SPLIT PEAS

Renowned for their sweet and nutty flavour, these make the most popular dhal in India, but are also widely used for tagines in Moroccan cookery. Split peas are made from splitting a small relative of the chickpea in half. They are not ideal for salads as they tend to become too mushy.

DO THEY NEED SOAKING? **NO**
COOKING **30–40 MINUTES AT A SIMMER**
BUY DRIED

SPROUTING PULSES

The process of watching dried, lifeless beans sprout is truly uplifting. The result is a really digestible, healthy ingredient that is bliss when added to salad leaves or served as the crunch in a sandwich. Sprouted pulses are available in many supermarkets and health food shops but they are easy (and far more cost effective) to make at home. Here's how:

All you need are some beans (nearly all can be used except kidney and soya beans that contain a toxin that is destroyed by cooking), a perfectly clean jar to sprout them in and some netting or muslin secured around the top of the jar, allowing the water to drain. Add your chosen bean to the jar, pour over water covering 3–5cm above the beans and allow them to soak overnight. The following day, drain the water and rinse the beans until the water runs clear. Now simply leave the jar at an angle to let it drain and allow air to circulate, undisturbed. Rinse the beans in fresh water, daily, for 1–4 days until the little sprouts wake and spring into life. Use as you like.

It is worth noting that mung beans, lentils and chickpeas are all quick to grow (take 2-3 days on average) but a larger bean like a butter bean may take 4 days.

....

white

BUTTER BEANS

✳

CANNELLINI BEANS

✳

HARICOT BEANS

✳

GIGANTE BEANS

white bean & pesto pizza

FOR THE PIZZA BASES
360ml warm water
2 x 7g sachets of dried yeast
   or 30g fresh yeast
2 teaspoons caster sugar
700g strong bread flour, plus
   extra for dusting
2 teaspoons salt
50ml olive oil, plus extra for
   greasing

FOR THE PESTO
50g pine nuts
70g basil, leaves only, plus
   extra to garnish
2 fat garlic cloves, crushed
50g Parmesan, grated
200ml olive oil
A squeeze of lemon juice
Sea salt

FOR THE WHITE BEAN PASTE
10g butter
2 shallots, chopped
Sprig of rosemary, chopped
400g can cannellini beans,
   drained and rinsed
50ml olive oil
Salt and freshly ground
   black pepper

This is a lovely vegetarian recipe prompted by a Venetian way of serving pizza with straightforward pesto. Once the white bean paste and pesto are made, they are simply dolloped over fresh dough with mozzarella and basil and baked.

PREP TIME 45 MINUTES + PROVING ✳ **COOK TIME 12 MINUTES** ✳ **MAKES 4 PIZZAS**

Start by making the pizza bases. Measure half the water (180ml) into a small bowl and sprinkle over the yeast and sugar. Stir to blend and set aside for 5–10 minutes until the surface is a little foamy. This proves the yeast is active.

Sift the flour and salt into a large bowl and make a well in the centre. Pour in the yeast mixture, oil and the remaining warm water. Mix well using your hands and add a little more flour if the dough seems too wet, or a touch more water if it seems too dry. Transfer the dough to a lightly floured surface and knead for 8–10 minutes until soft and elastic. Return the dough to a clean, oiled bowl and cover with a damp tea towel or oiled clingfilm. Leave in a warm place for about 1½ hours until doubled in size.

Meanwhile, make the pesto. Toast the pine nuts in a dry frying pan until golden then tip into a food processor or blender with the basil leaves, garlic and Parmesan. Blitz to a paste then, using the pulse setting, trickle in the olive oil. Season to taste with salt and fresh lemon juice.

For the white bean paste, melt the butter in a small frying pan over a medium heat. Add the shallots and gently fry for 3–4 minutes until softened. Add the chopped rosemary and cannellini beans and continue to cook for 4 minutes until piping hot and beginning to sweat a little. Empty into a bowl and add the olive oil. Using a hand-held blender, whizz to a coarse paste and season.

Preheat the oven to 220°C/200°C fan/gas mark 7. Place a baking sheet in the oven to get really hot – this will give you a crisp base. Knock back the dough by kneading it again for a minute or so, then divide into four equal pieces. Using a well-floured rolling pin, roll out each ball of dough as thinly as possible. Remove the baking sheet from the oven, dust it with flour before carefully transferring the dough base onto it. Spread over about 5 tablespoons of the pesto. Then dollop with white bean paste, again, about 5 tablespoons and cook for 10–12 minutes. Repeat for the other pizzas. Garnish with fresh basil, season with black pepper and serve immediately.

white bean & spinach tarts with a nut crust

FOR THE TART CRUST
125g hazelnuts, skin on
125g whole blanched
   almonds
1 teaspoon dukkah
1 tablespoon olive oil, plus
   extra for greasing
1 medium egg

FOR THE FILLING
100g young-leaf spinach
400g can white beans, such
   as cannellini
2 tablespoons crème fraîche
1 medium egg, beaten
1 garlic clove, crushed
salt and freshly ground
   black pepper

No pastry here, just a sticky crumb made by whizzing nuts with a little butter and egg. Rather than rolling the crust, press it into the tin and smooth it down using damp fingers before baking blind. The soft, beany filling sits well within the nutty crust, but be sure to drizzle over good-quality olive oil before serving.

PREP TIME 30 MINUTES ✳ COOK TIME 40 MINUTES ✳ MAKES 4

Preheat the oven to 180°C/160°C fan/gas mark 4. For the crust, put the hazelnuts, almonds, dukkah, oil and egg into a food processor and process, scraping down the sides occasionally, for 3–4 minutes until the mixture is fine and comes together. Press into four lightly greased 10cm loose-bottomed tart tins, pushing the crust up the sides to create an edge. Try to get the crust to the thickness of a pound coin (about 0.25cm). Refrigerate for 20 minutes, then prick the bases with a fork. Place on a large baking sheet and cook for 15 minutes, or until lightly golden and domed. Set aside to cool.

Meanwhile, make the filling. Wilt the spinach by placing the leaves in a sieve or colander. Pour over boiling water, about 1 litre, until the leaves wane. Squeeze any excess water from them, then roughly chop. Whizz the beans using a handheld blender or food processor and once smooth, combine with the crème fraîche, egg and garlic. Stir through the chopped spinach. Season the mixture and dollop into the cooled tart cases.

Return to the oven for a further 20–25 minutes until the filling has only just set. Remove before you see any cracks appear. Allow to cool slightly, then remove the tarts from the tins. Serve with fresh green leaves.

bright green mackerel with butter beans & courgettes

INGREDIENTS

2 tablespoons olive oil

5 shallots, sliced

3 garlic cloves, sliced

150g tenderstem broccoli

2 x 400g cans butter beans, drained and rinsed

2 courgettes, grated

75ml vegetable stock

100ml double cream

10g basil, torn

4 mackerel fillets, bones removed but skin on

A little plain flour, seasoned

Mackerel in all its forms, whether smoked, fried or served as pickled sashimi, is a phenomenal choice of fish. A combination of the intense taste and assurance that plenty of healthy oils and omega-3 are hitting our system is a strong backbone to any recipe.

PREP TIME 20 MINUTES ✳ COOK TIME 45 MINUTES ✳ SERVES 6

Preheat the oven to 180°C/160°C fan/gas mark 4.

Heat half the olive oil in a medium, deep-sided frying pan over a high heat. Fry the shallots and garlic for 3–4 minutes until golden. Remove from the heat and set aside.

Bring a small saucepan of water to the boil and add the broccoli. Simmer for 5–6 minutes until the broccoli has just started to soften. Drain and set aside.

Transfer the softened shallots and garlic to a large mixing bowl. Add the cooked broccoli, butter beans, courgettes, stock, cream and half the basil and mix well. Spoon into a large ovenproof dish, cover with foil and bake for 30 minutes until all is heated through and gloriously bubbly.

A few minutes before the end of the cooking time, focus on the mackerel. Dip the skin side of each fillet into the seasoned flour to lightly coat. Heat the remaining oil in the frying pan. Gently place the mackerel fillets in the hot pan, skin-side down. Turn the mackerel after just 2 or 3 minutes, when you can see that the flesh is cooked halfway up the fillet. Cook on the other side for a further 2 minutes.

Serve the fried fish on top of a pile of hot beans garnished with some basil.

✳TIP

Dry the mackerel fillets with kitchen paper before you add them to the frying pan – this gives you the best chance of crispy skin.

lamb stew with artichokes & cannellini beans

INGREDIENTS

3 tablespoons olive oil
900g lamb shoulder, cut into 3cm cubes
1 large onion, sliced
4 garlic cloves, thinly sliced
125ml white wine
1 tablespoon tomato purée
2 tablespoons white wine vinegar
300ml hot vegetable stock
Sprig of rosemary
400g artichoke hearts, chargrilled or in brine, drained
Zest and juice of 1 lemon (you need 2 tablespoons)
400g can cannellini beans, drained and rinsed
100g sun-dried tomatoes, roughly chopped
2 tablespoons chopped flat-leaf parsley
Salt and freshly ground black pepper

A hands-off stew that nods towards the Mediterranean with its sun-dried tomato, rosemary and lemon notes. Carry on cooking until the lamb gives under the pressure of a fork, tweaking the timings until the consistency feels right.

PREP TIME 30 MINUTES ✳ **COOK TIME 3 HOURS** ✳ **SERVES 6**

Heat half the oil in a large frying pan over a high heat. Brown the lamb in batches until all the pieces are well coloured on all sides. Take your time doing this and you will be able to taste the extra layer of flavour. Remove the lamb from the pan and set aside.

Pour the remaining olive oil into the pan and add the onion with a pinch of salt and sauté, over a medium heat, stirring frequently until it is golden, soft and sticky. Add the garlic and cook for 2 minutes until soft. Pour over the wine and allow it to reduce by two-thirds, until the liquid has almost evaporated.

Transfer the lamb, onion, garlic and reduced wine into a 2-litre heavy-based casserole dish. Stir through the tomato purée, vinegar and stock. Tuck in the rosemary sprig and season the stew generously. Cover with a tight-fitting lid and cook over a low heat for 3 hours, stirring from time to time. If it seems to need more liquid add a splash of water.

Remove the lid and stir through the artichokes, lemon juice and cannellini beans. Replace the lid and gently cook for a further 15 minutes, then spoon through the sun-dried tomatoes.

Serve at once, topped with the lemon zest, parsley and a grinding of black pepper.

pasta e fagioli with chicory

FOR THE BEANS

250g dried haricot beans, soaked overnight

3 bay leaves

1 whole dried chipotle chilli

Sprig of rosemary

1 Parmesan rind

1 carrot, scrubbed

2 celery sticks

FOR THE SOUP

3 tablespoons olive oil

1 large onion, roughly chopped

3 garlic cloves, finely chopped

400g can good-quality chopped tomatoes

200ml dry white wine

125g dried pasta of your choice (my favourite is rigatoni)

½ small head of chicory, finely sliced

Small handful of chopped basil

Salt and freshly ground black pepper

Freshly grated Parmesan, to serve

An aged Italian recipe full of tradition that, like many a successful recipe, started out as peasant fodder. The heady flavour and commonly found ingredients mean this dish comes together with ease, over gentle, slow cooking. Keep simmering until the beans are soft – this may mean slightly adapting the timings as each pot will cook differently.

PREP TIME 20 MINUTES + OVERNIGHT SOAKING
✳ **COOK TIME 2 HOURS 35 MINUTES** ✳ **SERVES 6**

Start by making the beans. Rinse the soaked beans and put them into a large, heavy-based pan. Cover with cold salted water (twice the volume of water to beans). Throw in the aromatics – the bay leaves, chilli, rosemary, cheese rind, carrot and celery – and bring the water to the boil. Turn down the heat and simmer, uncovered, until the beans are tender – about 1½–2 hours. Remove the pan from the heat and leave to stand for 20 minutes. Remove the herbs, cheese rind and vegetables (but not the beans) using a slotted spoon and discard.

While the beans are resting, work on the soup. Heat the oil in a large, deep saucepan over a medium heat. Add the onion and garlic and fry for about 5 minutes until soft and a nutty brown colour. Add the tomatoes and continue to cook, stirring frequently, for 10–12 minutes until any excess liquid has completely reduced. Pour in the wine and bring to the boil, simmering for a further 5 minutes until it has almost all evaporated.

Add the rested beans and their cooking liquor to the pan and continue cooking for a few minutes over a medium heat until all is nicely combined. Stir through the dried pasta, add enough cold water to cover the pasta by 2–3cm and simmer for 15 minutes until the pasta is al dente. Season to taste then spoon into bowls and top with the chicory and basil. Place a bowl of grated Parmesan on the table for people to help themselves.

cheese & cannellini bean pie with fennel seed pastry

FOR THE PASTRY

150g unsalted butter, chilled, plus extra for greasing

400g plain flour, sifted, plus extra for dusting

½ teaspoon salt

¼ teaspoon mustard powder

1½ teaspoons fennel seeds

1 egg, beaten with a little milk, for glazing

FOR THE FILLING

1 medium (250g) King Edward potato, peeled and cut into small cubes

30g unsalted butter

4 large (200g) banana shallots, sliced

Small bunch of spring onions, sliced

2 medium eggs

130ml double cream

2 tablespoons roughly chopped flat-leaf parsley

200g mature Cheddar, grated

400g can cannellini beans, drained and rinsed

Salt and freshly ground black pepper

Perhaps it is because my brother makes pies for a living that I have developed quite a cook's snobbishness towards them! The pastry must be a trusted, faithful recipe that can cope, neigh support, the filling. Use a strong Cheddar as the beans work well with punchy flavours.

PREP TIME 40 MINUTES + 30 MINUTES CHILLING
✳ **COOK TIME 1 HOUR** ✳ **SERVES 6**

First make the pie filling. Boil the potato in a large saucepan of salted water for 10–15 minutes until a knife is easily inserted but the cubes are still holding their shape. Drain and set aside.

Meanwhile, gently melt the butter in a small saucepan over a low heat and gently sweat the shallots and spring onions until softened but not coloured, stirring occasionally for about 10 minutes. Remove from the heat and set aside. Lightly whisk together the eggs, cream, parsley and cheese. Add a healthy pinch of salt and a grinding of black pepper. Set aside.

For the pastry, put the butter and 110ml cold water in a small saucepan and heat until melted, then bring to a simmer. Tip the flour, salt, mustard powder and fennel seeds into the molten mixture. Working quickly, stir until the mixture comes together and a soft dough is formed. Gather the warm dough together and form into a disc. Wrap in clingfilm and chill for 30 minutes.

Preheat the oven to 180°C/160°C fan/gas mark 4 and grease a large pie dish (about 26cm in diameter).

On a lightly floured work surface, roll out two-thirds of the pastry big enough to line the base and sides of your pie dish. Roll out the remaining pastry to create a lid. Carefully lower the rolled pastry into the dish to form the base.

Mix together the cannellini beans, potatoes, shallot mixture and beaten egg mixture. Spoon into the pastry-lined dish. Cover the pie with the pastry lid and seal by crimping the edges decoratively. Glaze the top of the pie with the egg and milk mixture. Poke a couple of small steam holes in the top, then chill the pie for 10 minutes. Cook for 40–45 minutes until golden brown and serve.

beef pie with a cannellini bean & parsnip crust

INGREDIENTS

2 tablespoons olive oil
2 large leeks, diced
2 carrots, cut into small
  cubes
2 garlic cloves, crushed
475g lean beef mince
2 tablespoons tomato purée
1 tablespoon plain flour
1 tablespoon finely chopped
  mint
2 tablespoons finely
  chopped flat-leaf parsley
½ can (200g) chopped
  tomatoes or passata
250ml hot beef stock

FOR THE TOPPING

350g parsnips, peeled and
  cut into quarters
Generous knob of butter
2 x 400g cans cannellini
  beans, drained and rinsed
4 tablespoons soured cream
2 tablespoons olive oil
½ garlic clove, grated
50g mature Cheddar, grated
30g pumpkin seeds
Salt and freshly ground
  black pepper

I tend to serve this for a large gathering, made in advance and stored, covered, in the fridge for a day or two before being needed. The topping is surprising as it's made without potato, but this offers depth and interest to the pie. Be sure to cook the filling slowly, and add just enough liquid to make it soft but not soupy.

PREP TIME 30 MINUTES ✳ COOK TIME 1 HOUR 30 MINUTES ✳ SERVES 4 GENEROUSLY

Heat half the oil in a large heavy-based casserole dish over a medium heat. Add the leeks and carrots and cook gently, for about 10 minutes, until they have softened and the leeks are translucent. Add the garlic and cook for a further minute. Remove the vegetables from the pan and set aside. Add the remaining oil to the pan with the beef mince and fry over a high heat until the meat has taken on a little colour. Return the softened vegetables to the pan and stir through the tomato purée, flour and herbs. Cook slightly before pouring in the tomatoes or passata and stock. Bring to the boil, then turn down the heat to a simmer and cook for about 40 minutes until the liquid has reduced by half and the ingredients have come together.

Preheat the oven to 200°C/180°C fan/gas mark 6.

Meanwhile, make the topping. Bring a large saucepan of water to the boil and add the parsnips. Boil for 15–20 minutes until they are soft and mashable. Drain and tip back into the pan. Add the butter and the beans and return the pan to the heat. Cook for about 5 minutes before stirring through the soured cream, oil and garlic. Remove from the heat and mash until you have spoonable consistency, adding a little more soured cream if needed. Season to taste.

Spoon the filling into a 1.5 litre ovenproof pie dish. Spread over the topping and press down with a fork. Sprinkle with the cheese and pumpkin seeds and bake for 25–30 minutes, then finish by putting the pie under the grill for a further 5 minutes until the topping is lovely and brown.

spiced bean potato cakes with soft poached eggs

INGREDIENTS

600g floury potatoes,
  unpeeled
400g can haricot beans,
  drained and rinsed
A glug of olive oil
1 banana shallot or 2 round
  shallots, finely sliced
1 garlic clove, crushed
1 heaped teaspoon turmeric
  powder
1 teaspoon caraway seeds
½ teaspoon Kashmiri chilli
  powder
Small bunch of coriander,
  chopped
Juice of ½ lemon
3 tablespoons chickpea
  (gram) flour
3–4 tablespoons vegetable
  oil
Seasoned plain flour, to coat
Salt and freshly ground
  black pepper

FOR THE TOPPING

4 large eggs
1 tablespoon chopped
  coriander

These little potato and Indian-spiced patties considerably improve a breakfast table. The addition of gram flour is a must as it acts as an ideal thickening ingredient. You can make the potoato cakes the day before, but they might just need a touch longer in the oven.

PREP TIME 40 MINUTES + 30 MINUTES CHILLING
✳ **COOK TIME 20–30 MINUTES** ✳ **SERVES 4 GENEROUSLY**

Boil the potatoes whole in lightly salted water until just tender, remove from the heat and drain. Set aside to steam-dry for at least 10 minutes. Once cool enough to handle, rub off the skins. Roughly chop half the potatoes and set aside. Add the haricot beans to the remaining potatoes and mash using the back of a fork until you have a slightly chunky mash consistency.

Heat half the oil in a frying pan over a medium–low heat, add the shallot and cook for 4–5 minutes until lightly brown. Add the garlic and cook for 1 minute. Stir through the spices and cook for a further 3 minutes. Set aside.

Add the shallot and spice mixture, the coriander, lemon juice and the chickpea flour to the lightly crushed potatoes and stir through, together with the reserved chopped potatoes. Season well with salt and a little black pepper. Use your hands to form into eight patties and chill for at least 30 minutes.

Preheat the oven to 200°C/180°C fan/gas mark 6.

Heat the remaining oil in a large non-stick frying pan over a medium heat. Dip the patties into a bowl of seasoned flour, brushing off any excess. Add them to the pan and cook for 5–6 minutes until a golden brown crust forms on the base. Carefully turn over the potato cakes and cook for a further 5 minutes. Transfer to a baking tray and cook in the oven for 10–12 minutes.

Meanwhile, poach the eggs. Bring a large saucepan of water to a simmer. Make a whirlpool in the centre by stirring rapidly with the handle of a wooden spoon. When the whirlpool has almost completely subsided, crack the eggs directly into it. Poach for 2½–3 minutes over a gentle heat. Place a poached egg on each potato cake and sprinkle with chopped coriander.

Tuscan kale ragout

INGREDIENTS

300g dried giant Spanish butter beans (gigante), soaked overnight and drained, or 2 x 400g cans butter beans, drained and rinsed

FOR THE PARSLEY OIL

100ml extra virgin olive oil
2 fat garlic cloves, peeled
Medium bunch of parsley, leaves picked
Pinch of sugar
30g Parmesan, finely grated
Juice of ½ small lemon
Salt and freshly ground black pepper

FOR THE RAGOUT

2 tablespoons olive oil
1 large onion, chopped
2 garlic cloves, roughly chopped
2 celery stalks, sliced into thin crescents
1 large fennel bulb, fronds roughly chopped and the bulb cut into 3mm slices
4 bay leaves
200g kale, roughly chopped
Zest of 1 unwaxed lemon
400ml hot vegetable stock
30g dried breadcrumbs
30g Parmesan, finely grated

Ragout is a catch term for a slow-cooked, French-style stew. Here, gigante beans (or giant beans) are used, for visual impact as much as anything else. Swap with butter beans if preferred and serve with a green salad and a hunk of buttered bread.

PREP TIME 30 MINUTES + OVERNIGHT SOAKING
✳ **COOK TIME 1 HOUR 30 MINUTES** ✳ **SERVES 4**

If you are using dried, not canned, beans, rinse the soaked beans under cool, running water and put them in a large saucepan. Cover with fresh cold water and bring to a simmer. Cook, uncovered, occasionally skimming the surface, until the beans can be easily crushed with the back of a spoon. This will take about 1 hour but check after 45 minutes. Drain and season generously. If you are using canned butter beans, omit this step and simply season generously.

Prepare the parsley oil by blitzing the oil, garlic, parsley, sugar, Parmesan and lemon juice using a blender or hand-held mixer. Stir through 50–70ml of cold water to create a loose paste. Season to taste. Scrape into a small bowl and set aside.

Preheat the oven to 200°C/180°C fan/gas mark 6.

To make the ragout, heat the oil with a pinch of salt in a large saucepan over a medium–low heat. Add the onion, garlic, celery, sliced fennel and fronds. Cover the pan and cook for 10–15 minutes, stirring occasionally, until all the vegetables have gently relaxed. Stir the bay leaves and cooked beans into the softened mixture and mix well. Add the kale and lemon zest. Pour over the hot vegetable stock and combine. Continue to cook for 4–5 minutes until the kale has wilted.

Decant the ragout into a deep-sided 2-litre ovenproof dish. Swirl through the parsley oil and season for a second time. Sprinkle over the breadcrumbs and Parmesan. Transfer to the oven and bake, uncovered, for 35–40 minutes until bubbling. Allow the ragout to rest slightly briefly before serving.

*TIP

If you don't have time to
soak dried butter beans
overnight, put them into
a very large saucepan,
cover generously with cold
water and bring to the
boil. Simmer for a good 10
minutes, skimming off the
foam with a large spoon
before removing the pan
from the heat and leaving
to stand for 3 hours. Drain
and continue from step 2.

butter bean, fig & anchovy on sourdough

INGREDIENTS

4 large slices of sourdough
1–2 tablespoons olive oil
1 garlic clove, halved
1 banana shallot, finely diced
4–5 sage leaves, finely sliced
5–6 salted anchovy fillets,
  finely chopped
400g can butter beans,
  drained and rinsed
160ml single cream

TO SERVE

4 small, soft figs, halved or
  sliced
Handful of green leaves

This is a brilliant, mid-week recipe when you don't have much time on your hands. The lion's share of ingredients might be found in your storecupboard and the whole thing should be on the table within 15 minutes. The salty anchovy/ cream combination gets me every time – throw in some smooth butter beans and fresh figs and it becomes heaven on a plate.

PREP TIME 10 MINUTES ✳ **COOK TIME 15 MINUTES**
✳ **SERVES 2 GENEROUSLY**

Brush the sourdough on both sides with a little of the oil. Be wary, the bread will drink up the oil, so try not to use too much. Heat a large frying pan over a medium–high heat and, when hot, fry the slices until toasted on both sides. Depending on the size of your pan, this may need to be done in batches. As you remove the sourdough slices from the pan, immediately rub one side with the garlic clove.

Add the remaining oil to the frying pan and return it to a medium heat. Add the shallot and sage leaves and fry for 3–4 minutes until the shallot is soft and golden. Stir through the anchovy fillets and cook for a further minute.

Stir the beans into the anchovy mix along with the single cream, and keep over a very gentle heat until you are ready to serve, adding a touch of water if the mixture becomes too dry.

Top the sourdough with the warm butter bean mixture and serve with the figs and seasonal green leaves.

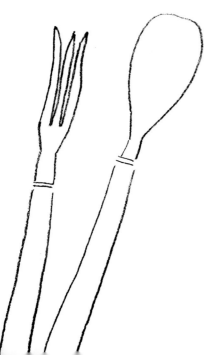

pumpkin & butter bean soup with fennel sausage

INGREDIENTS

1 tablespoon olive oil

1 blue pumpkin or butternut squash (approx. 900g–1kg), peeled and cut into small cubes

3 celery sticks, finely chopped

2 large shallots, finely chopped

1 garlic clove, crushed

2 x 400g cans butter beans, drained and rinsed

1 litre hot vegetable stock

FOR THE FENNEL SAUSAGE

½ tablespoon olive oil

½ teaspoon fennel seeds, lightly bashed

2 pork sausages, skins removed

50ml double cream

Zest of 1 and juice of 2 oranges

Dill fronds, to garnish

Salt and freshly ground black pepper

Soup has always been in my weekly repertoire. While others might plump for a heartier pasta or meat, I genuinely relish the thought of a deep bowl of hot soup. Substitute pumpkin for squash, if that is easier, although you can't beat the sweet, earthy, soft taste of in-season pumpkin.

PREP TIME 25 MINUTES ✳ COOK TIME 45 MINUTES ✳ SERVES 6

Start by making the soup. Heat the oil in a large heavy-based casserole dish over a medium heat. Add the pumpkin, celery and shallots and gently sweat for 10 minutes until the vegetables are slightly softened – try not to colour them at this stage. Add the garlic and cook for a further minute before adding the rinsed butter beans and vegetable stock. Cover the pan and cook gently for 30–35 minutes until all the vegetables are tender and breaking apart.

Meanwhile, prepare the fennel sausage. Heat the oil in a frying pan over a medium heat. Add the fennel seeds and cook gently for 1 minute, or until beginning to pop. Add the sausage meat to the pan and use a wooden spoon to break up the meat. Fry gently until the sausage meat turns a rich golden brown. Set aside.

Blitz the soup using a free-standing or hand-held blender until it has a smooth, silky consistency. Add the cream, orange zest and juice, then stir to combine and season to taste.

Return the soup to the casserole dish over a medium heat and gently reheat. Divide the soup between warmed bowls and top each one with the crumbled fennel sausage and a few dill fronds.

bacon baked beans with crusty breadcrumbs

INGREDIENTS

400g dried haricot beans, soaked overnight and drained
1 large onion, cut in half
2 fresh bay leaves
5 black peppercorns
75ml white wine
100g brown sugar
1 tablespoon black treacle
½ tablespoon chilli flakes
½ teaspoon cumin
1 teaspoon salt
2 tablespoons tomato purée
1 tablespoon Worcestershire sauce
1 tablespoon Dijon mustard
200g lardons
150g fresh breadcrumbs
40g butter

The pairing of beans sitting in a thick sauce has long made good sense and seems to satisfy both children and adults alike. The breadcrumbs are a welcome addition, giving the dish extra body and another layer of flavour. If you have any left over, these beans will only improve with flavour over the course of a few days.

PREP TIME 20 MINUTES + OVERNIGHT SOAKING ✳ COOK TIME 3 HOURS
✳ SERVES 6–8

Put the haricot beans, onion, bay leaves and peppercorns in a 2-litre ovenproof casserole or stockpot and cover with 1.5 litres of cold water. Simmer, uncovered, for about 50 minutes – 1 hour, or until the beans are just tender. Drain the beans but reserve 600ml of the cooking water. Remove and discard the halved onion and bay leaves.

Rinse out the casserole and add the wine, sugar, black treacle, chilli flakes, cumin, salt, tomato purée, Worcestershire sauce, mustard and the reserved 600ml of cooking water. Heat until bubbling and cook over a medium heat for a few minutes until the sauce has come together. Add the beans to the sauce along with the lardons.

Preheat the oven to 180°C/160°C fan/gas mark 4.

Put the lid on the casserole, transfer to the oven and cook for 1½ hours until the beans are soft enough to squash between your fingers and the sauce has become syrupy. Remove the lid and sprinkle over the breadcrumbs. Place small knobs of butter over the breadcrumbs and return to the oven, uncovered, for about 30 minutes, or until the topping is golden and bubbling.

crushed avocado, burrata & butter beans on toast

INGREDIENTS
A glug of olive oil
400g can butter beans, drained and rinsed
2 large ripe avocados, halved, peeled and roughly chopped
Zest and juice of 1 lime
2 tablespoons roughly chopped coriander
Pinch of Maldon sea salt
1 garlic clove, sliced in half
4 slices of sourdough bread
200g burrata or soft mozzarella cheese, torn into pieces
Olive oil, to serve

The avocados you choose here is the key to this recipe's success. You want them at their peak – ripe, but not too soft. Burrata is really a superior, often slightly larger, version of mozzarella, but it has a far softer creamy core. You should be able to find it quite easily in cheese shops or some supermarkets.

PREP TIME 10 MINUTES ✳ **COOK TIME 5 MINUTES** ✳ **SERVES 4**

Heat the oil in a small saucepan over a medium heat, then add the beans and warm through for 1–2 minutes. Remove from the heat and lightly mash using a potato masher, adding a little more oil or warm water if needed. It looks nice to leave one or two butter beans whole rather than reduce them all to a mash.

Put the avocado flesh in a small bowl with the lime juice and gently mash with a fork. Stir through the coriander and most of lime zest (reserve a little to garnish). Season with sea salt.

Toast or grill the soughdough slices when you are ready to serve. Rub the garlic clove over the slices and top each with the beans, some mashed avocado, burrata, the reserved lime zest and a drizzle of oil. Serve straight away.

pork belly with apple & butter bean purée & fennel

INGREDIENTS

1 piece of pork belly (about
   1.3–1.4 kg)
2 teaspoons sea salt
Sprig of rosemary, finely
   chopped
A small glug of olive oil
4 banana shallots, quartered
2 large fennel bulbs,
   trimmed and quartered
150ml cider

FOR THE PURÉE

300g dried butter beans,
   soaked overnight and
   drained
1 Cox's apple, peeled and cut
   into cubes
2 garlic cloves, crushed
1 tablespoon cider vinegar
130ml olive oil, plus extra
   to drizzle
2 tablespoons lemon juice
½ bunch flat-leaf parsley,
   finely chopped
Sea salt and freshly ground
   black pepper

The combination of pork, apple and fennel has long been recognised as a frontrunner in flavour. If you get it right, the slow-cooked meat is served soft and falling apart, the crackling crisp and the purée soft.

PREP TIME 45 MINUTES + OVERNIGHT SOAKING
✳ **COOK TIME 2 HOURS 30 MINUTES** ✳ **SERVES 6**

Preheat the oven to 220°C/200°C fan/gas mark 7. Select a roasting dish large enough for the pork belly to lie flat.

Use a sharp knife, score the skin of the pork belly in diagonal lines about 2.5cm apart, taking care to score the fat and not cut into the meat. Rub the salt and rosemary deep into the fat and season with pepper. Drizzle with the oil. Place the belly in the roasting dish and roast for 30 minutes. The skin will start to crackle. Reduce the heat to 180°C/160°C fan/gas mark 4 and roast for a further hour. Remove from the oven and place the belly on a board. Tip the shallots and fennel into the roasting tin and smother with molten fat. Place the pork back on top. Pour the cider around the belly, taking care not to pour any on the crackling, and roast for a final hour. It is ready when the meat is deliciously tender, almost falling apart, and the crackling is crispy. Rest for 10 minutes.

Meanwhile, make the purée. Put the butter beans in a large saucepan and cover with fresh water. Bring to the boil over a medium heat, then reduce the heat and simmer for 40–45 minutes until the beans begin to soften.

Put the apple, garlic and cider vinegar in a small saucepan over a medium heat. Cover with a tight-fitting lid and cook for 5 minutes until almost all the liquid has evaporated and the apple begins to soften. Set aside.

Drain the beans, reserving some of the cooking water, then tip into a food-processor. Add the apple, oil, lemon juice and blend, with a little cooking water, to create a loose purée. Season to taste and stir through the chopped parsley.

Slice the pork into six portions. Pile up the butter bean purée with the fennel and shallots. Top with the sliced pork and serve with a final drizzle of olive oil.

lemon, blueberry & butter bean cake

INGREDIENTS

400g can butter beans,
  drained and rinsed
50ml olive oil, plus extra
  for greasing
3 medium eggs
Zest and juice of 2
  unwaxed lemons
100g caster sugar
150g ground almonds
90g fine polenta
1 teaspoon baking powder
200g blueberries

FOR THE SYRUP

Juice of 1 large lemon
50g caster sugar

A citrussy, filling loaf with a wonderfully thick texture that should be brought to the table in slabs. I'm sure it will be wolfed down in one tea sitting, warm from the oven, with a blob of yogurt or indeed nothing at all. What's more, it's gluten- and dairy-free.

PREP TIME 20 MINUTES ✳ COOK TIME 45 MINUTES ✳ MAKES 1 X 900G LOAF

Preheat the oven to 180°C/160°C fan/gas mark 4. Grease a 900g loaf tin with oil and line it with baking parchment.

Put the beans and oil in the bowl of a food processor and blitz to a thick paste. Scrape this into a mixing bowl and stir through the eggs, one at a time, and mix well before adding the lemon zest and juice, sugar, almonds, polenta and baking powder.

Pour half the batter into the tin, scatter with half the blueberries before topping with the remaining batter. Sprinkle the remaining blueberries over the top, lightly pressing them into the batter. Bake for 45 minutes.

Meanwhile, make a syrup by warming the lemon juice and sugar with 1 tablespoon of water in a small saucepan.

As soon as the cake is cooked, remove it from the oven and immediately pour the syrup over it while still in the tin. Don't worry if it collects in the corners slightly; it will soak into the sponge. Allow to cool a little before removing from the tin. Serve in slices.

black

BLACK BEANS

✳

BLACK-EYED BEANS

✳

PUY LENTILS

✳

BLACK BELUGA LENTILS

raw broccoli, black bean & spring onion salad

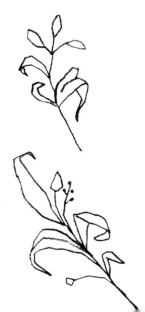

INGREDIENTS

40g unsalted butter
1 teaspoon mustard seeds
½ teaspoon paprika
400g can black beans,
 drained and rinsed
2 tablespoons olive oil
1 tablespoon cider vinegar
5 spring onions, finely sliced
150g broccoli, 1–2cm
 trimmed from the base
50g lamb's lettuce
½ green chilli, finely
 chopped
Salt

TO GARNISH

50g sunflower seeds, toasted
Plenty of cracked black
 pepper

Food should make you feel good and, to me, a well-balanced salad is perfection. Sitting down to a lunch of uncomplicated, crisp, freshly prepared food sets off afternoons that promise to be fruitful, energetic ones. I'll often make a variant of this; we always have broccoli in the fridge and eating it raw is my favourite. The beans are warmed slightly in spiced butter, which becomes the dressing.

PREP TIME 15 MINUTES ✳ COOK TIME 10 MINUTES ✳ SERVES 6

Melt the butter in a medium frying pan over a medium heat, then add the mustard seeds. Cook for 1–2 minutes before adding the paprika and black beans. Continue to cook for 4–5 minutes. Season well with salt and remove from the heat. Stir through the oil and cider vinegar. The liquid will become the dressing, so add a little more oil if your beans drink up the liquid.

To assemble the salad, slice each broccoli floret as thinly as you are able to and place in a large bowl. The little green fronds tend to come apart from the 'trees'; simply add them to the bowl too. Gently combine with the lamb's lettuce and green chilli. Spoon over the warm black bean mix, juices and all, and transfer the salad to a generous platter. Garnish with the sunflower seeds and cracked black pepper.

black bean dhal

INGREDIENTS

350g dried black beans,
  soaked overnight
  and drained
2 teaspoons cumin seeds
1 teaspoon coriander seeds
2 tablespoons olive oil
1 onion, finely chopped
6 curry leaves
2 garlic cloves, sliced
5cm piece of ginger, peeled
  and finely chopped
1 teaspoon chilli powder
2 teaspoons garam masala
2 teaspoons smoked paprika
400g can chopped tomatoes
1 green chilli, halved
1 cinnamon stick
Sea salt

Plain naan or flatbreads,
  warmed, to serve

I remember enduring an eight-hour bus journey in Southern India, struggling with nausea, unrelenting dusty heat and greasy leopard-print seat covers. Nearing dusk we stopped in a lay-by for fresh air and my new husband intrepidly dodged headlights to cross the road to a tiny street-food stall. He proudly brought back our dinner – a sloppy, silky, spicy pile of black bean dhal served on a plastic plate. I still remember its soft, deep flavour and how we relished it. This recipe derives from those memories and could be eaten just as it is, with a cold corner of butter gently melting in the centre.

PREP TIME 20 MINUTES + OVERNIGHT SOAKING
✳ **COOK TIME 2 HOURS 50 MINUTES** ✳ **SERVES 6**

Put the beans into a large saucepan of cold water and bring to a rolling boil over a high heat. Once boiling, turn down the heat and simmer for 1 hour–1 hour 20 minutes, or until the beans are soft. Drain, return them to the pan and set aside.

Heat a small, dry frying pan and toast the cumin and coriander seeds for 2 minutes until just toasted. Crush lightly using a pestle and mortar (or, if easier, tip into a bowl and crush using the end of a rolling pin).

Heat the oil in a separate frying pan over a medium heat. Add the onion and curry leaves and fry gently for 5 minutes until soft and golden. Add the garlic and ginger and fry for a further few minutes. Stir in the cumin and coriander seeds, chilli powder, garam masala and paprika. Add the tomatoes and simmer for 2–3 minutes to warm through.

Add the onion and tomato mixture, green chilli, cinnamon stick and 200ml of cold water to the beans, stir then cover with a tight-fitting lid. Cook gently over a medium heat for 1 hour, stirring occasionally. Check the dhal at this point but expect to cook it for a further 20 minutes. Keep an eye on the liquid levels, topping up with a little water if the dhal becomes a little dry. Fish out the chilli and cinnamon stick and season with sea salt, to taste. Serve, in bowls, with plain naan or flatbreads.

rich tomato, black bean & nigella seed tart

FOR THE PASTRY

200g plain flour, plus extra
   for dusting
Pinch of salt
100g chilled butter, diced
30g Parmesan, grated
1 teaspoon nigella seeds
   (black onion seeds)
1 egg yolk
2–3 tablespoons ice-cold
   water

FOR THE FILLING

1 teaspoon mustard seeds
1 tablespoon olive oil
2 onions, peeled and sliced
3 garlic cloves
2 teaspoons brown sugar
75g tomato purée
3 eggs, lightly beaten
150ml single cream
400g can black beans,
   drained and rinsed
80g firm goat's cheese,
   sliced into rounds
1 teaspoon nigella seeds
   (black onion seeds)
Salt and freshly ground
   black pepper

Making tarts requires a little forethought, not least because they involve both a filling and a pastry step, but this pastry is a cinch – once you have made it two or three times your hands start to become familiar with a successful texture.

PREP TIME 40 MINUTES + 1 HOUR CHILLING
✳ COOK TIME 1 HOUR 10 MINUTES ✳ MAKES 1 x 30CM TART

For the pastry, sift the flour and salt into a large mixing bowl and add the butter. Using your fingertips and thumbs, lightly rub the butter into the flour mixture until the mixture resembles breadcrumbs. Add the Parmesan and nigella seeds and repeat until the cheese has been evenly incorporated. Now add the egg yolk and water and use a round-bladed knife to combine until the pastry comes together. Knead it very briefly so it forms a ball. Wrap the pastry in clingfilm and chill for 30 minutes. Don't be tempted to handle it too much, otherwise the fat will warm up and it will become tricky to handle.

Meanwhile, start making the filling. Add the mustard seeds to a dry frying pan over a high heat and toast for 1–2 minutes. Remove from the pan and set aside. Return the frying pan to a medium heat and pour in the oil, add the onions and fry until just soft, stirring regularly, before adding the garlic and cook for a final minute. Return the mustard seeds to the pan, spoon over the sugar and add the tomato purée. Reduce the heat to low and cook the mixture for 2–3 minutes. Remove from the heat and allow to cool slightly.

Lightly flour the work surface and roll out the pastry to the thickness of a £1 coin and use it to line the tart tin, ensuring the pastry edge stands just a little above the rim. Trim the edges, prick the base with a fork and return it to the fridge to chill for 30 minutes. Preheat the oven to 200°C/180°C fan/gas mark 6.

Continue with your filling. Combine the eggs, cream and the drained black beans in a bowl. Add the tomato-onion mixture, gently combine and season.

Line the tin with baking paper, fill with baking beans and bake for 20 minutes. Remove the paper and the beans and return to the oven for 5–8 minutes. Reduce the oven temperature to 190°C/170°C fan/gas mark 5. Pour in the filling, top with rounds of goat's cheese and the nigella seeds. Bake for 35 minutes or until just set. Allow to sit for 10–15 minutes before serving.

filo cigarettes with beetroot, lentils & caraway

INGREDIENTS

2 large beetroot (about
    325g), peeled and cut into
    1.5cm cubes
1 tablespoon olive oil
1 teaspoon caraway seeds,
    plus extra for sprinkling
2 garlic cloves, peeled
75g sourdough breadcrumbs
400g can black beluga
    lentils, drained
2 tablespoons Greek yogurt
Juice of ½ lemon
½ bunch of flat-leaf parsley,
    roughly chopped
7 sheets of filo pastry
    (roughly 30 x 40cm)
75g unsalted butter, melted
Salt and freshly ground
    black pepper

FOR THE DIP

200g Greek yogurt
2 tablespoons tahini
Juice of ½ lemon
1 teaspoon roughly chopped
    flat-leaf parsley

Commonly used in Greek and Middle-Eastern cuisines, filo pastry is a useful ingredient to become familiar with and can often help in hosting emergencies, so keep a pack in the freezer to pull out when needed. These simple rolls, stuffed with a roasted beetroot filling, are very good on their own, but the tahini yogurt turns them from picnic fodder to party food.

PREP TIME 30 MINUTES ✳ COOK TIME 50 MINUTES ✳ MAKES 21 CIGARETTES

Preheat the oven to 200°C/180°C fan/gas mark 6 and place a baking sheet in the oven to heat up – this will encourage the filo cigarettes to crisp up.

Put the beetroot in a small roasting tin and drizzle over the oil. Scatter with the caraway seeds and toss to combine. Roast for 20 minutes, turning once half-way through, until they are soft and deep purple in colour.

Tip the roasted beetroot, garlic, breadcrumbs, lentils, yogurt and lemon juice into the bowl of a food processor and pulse until you have a rough paste consistency. Season well and stir through the parsley.

Cut the filo sheets lengthways into 21 strips approximately 10 x 30cm. Brush each of the sheets with melted butter and place 2 teaspoons of the mixture at the base of each strip, along the short side. Roll up the strip to enclose the filling (the ends of the 'cigarette' can be left open) and place on the preheated baking sheet, lined with greaseproof paper. Finally, brush each completed roll with a little more melted butter and sprinkle over a few caraway seeds. Bake for 20–25 minutes or until the filo is golden.

To make the dip, combine the yogurt, tahini and lemon juice in a small bowl. Sprinkle with the parsley and serve alongside the beetroot-filled filo cigarettes.

soft polenta with mushroom black-eyed beans & spinach

INGREDIENTS

A knob of unsalted butter
A glug of olive oil
3 banana shallots, quartered
4 large chestnut mushrooms,
   cleaned and sliced
4 garlic cloves, sliced
125g young leaf spinach
400g can black-eyed beans,
   drained and rinsed
200ml hot vegetable stock
Salt and freshly ground
   black pepper

FOR THE POLENTA

1 litre vegetable stock
220g polenta
100ml single cream
50g butter
50g Parmesan, finely grated

This recipe requires little more than 20 minutes in front of the stove. The result is a swift, wintery, all-in-one number that should be eaten in shallow bowls sitting on the sofa with your best friends.

PREP TIME 20 MINUTES ✳ **COOK TIME 25 MINUTES** ✳ **SERVES 4**

Heat the butter and oil in a large heavy-based frying pan over a medium–high heat and add the shallots. Sauté for 5 minutes until soft before adding the mushrooms and garlic to the pan. It will be stuffed full but keep frying and within a few minutes, the mushrooms will shrink and everything will become manageable. Keeping the heat high, add the spinach and continue to heat until the leaves wilt. Finally, stir through the beans and stock. Season, turn down the heat to low and allow the sauce to simmer for a few minutes.

To make the polenta, bring the vegetable stock to the boil in a medium saucepan. Slowly pour in the polenta and stir as quickly as your wrist allows, removing any lumps that form. Bubble the polenta for a few minutes, stirring, until thickened. Remove the pan from the heat, stir in the cream, butter and Parmesan. Add plenty of seasoning and serve with the vegetables.

✳TIP

It is worth remembering that the longer you cook polenta the firmer it becomes, so be swift to serve this dish.

See page 52 for Softened Lentils with Fresh Dill Yogurt Cheese (pictured opposite)

softened lentils with fresh dill yogurt cheese

FOR THE DILL YOGURT CHEESE

1kg good-quality, full-fat natural yogurt

Zest of 1 lemon, plus a little extra to garnish

3 dill stalks, fronds only, finely chopped, plus a little extra to garnish

½ teaspoon cracked black peppercorns

Extra virgin olive oil, to preserve the labne

FOR THE LENTIL SALAD

2 tablespoons olive oil

1 teaspoon coriander seeds

1 teaspoon mustard seeds

3 small shallots, finely chopped

2 garlic cloves, sliced

200g dried black or Puy lentils, rinsed

400ml hot vegetable stock

A dash of red wine vinegar

Salt and freshly gound black pepper

You will also need a square of muslin for straining

The main ingredients here are humble enough – yogurt and lentils – but both have undergone some attention. The yogurt becomes a soft labne made by straining and rolling into a log shape then served, in slices, alongside a gently spiced lentil salad.

PREP TIME 15 MINUTES + 2 DAYS DRAINING ✳ COOK TIME 35 MINUTES ✳ SERVES 4

To make the cheese, tip the yogurt into a bowl and stir through the lemon zest and dill fronds. Grind in some cracked black pepper and gently combine everything together. Line a large sieve with a square of muslin and pour in the yogurt. Draw up and tie the edges of the cloth, enclosing the yogurt, and set the sieve over a bowl. Leave in the fridge to drain for two days. Gently squeeze out any excess liquid and open the muslin to reveal the yogurt cheese. Sprinkle dill fronds, lemon zest and black pepper over a length of clingfilm and tip the yogurt cheese onto the clingfilm. Using the clingfilm to help as a guide, roll tightly into a fat sausage shape. Refrigerate until needed.

Once the cheese is underway, prepare the lentil salad (it can also be made in advance and left to sit for a day or two in the fridge). Heat the oil a deep, heavy-based frying pan over a medium–high heat and add the coriander and mustard seeds. Fry the spices until sizzling, for about 1 minute, before adding the shallots and garlic to the pan. Sauté until just soft and stir through the lentils, coating them in the spiced onion mix. Pour over the vegetable stock and vinegar, lower the temperature to a simmer and cook for 25–30 minutes, or until the lentils are soft. Remove from the heat and allow to cool slightly before seasoning to taste.

Serve the lentils, warm or cold, with a slice of dill yogurt cheese.

chilaquiles with tomato salsa & jalapeño cream

INGREDIENTS

2 tablespoons vegetable oil
1 onion, finely chopped
2 garlic cloves, finely sliced
2 jalapeño peppers, finely
   sliced
1kg mixed tomatoes (green,
   yellow and red), roughly
   chopped
400g cooked black beluga
   lentils or black beans,
   drained and rinsed
Juice of 1 lime
150g tortilla chips
4 large eggs
Salt and freshly ground
   black pepper

FOR THE JALAPEÑO CREAM

100ml natural yogurt
200g ricotta cheese
3 jalapeño peppers, finely
   diced

TO SERVE

Lime wedges
Handful of coriander,
   roughly chopped

Mexican by origin, this is a colourful dish that I often serve for a family brunch – no surprises that my children like the thought of a meal that includes tortilla crisps. In short, a mildly spiced bright salsa is simmered before being poured over tortilla crisps and baked. The chilaquiles are served with a plethora of ricotta cream and hot fried eggs.

PREP TIME 25 MINUTES ✳ COOK TIME 25 MINUTES ✳ SERVES 4

Preheat oven to 170°C/150°C fan/gas mark 3.

Heat half the oil in a large ovenproof frying pan over a medium heat and fry the onion until just crispy. Add the garlic and jalapeño peppers and continue to fry for about 1 minute. Keeping the heat constant, pour the tomatoes and all their juice into the pan and cook for about 8 minutes until the tomatoes are beginning to collapse but still retain some structure. Stir through the beans, squeeze over the lime juice and season generously. Top with the tortilla chips and transfer the pan to the oven. Cook for 10 minutes.

Meanwhile, make the jalapeño cream. Put the yogurt and ricotta in a small bowl with the jalapeño peppers. Combine with a firm hand, working the ingredients for about 1 minute.

Heat the remaining oil in a separate frying pan and crack the eggs into the pan. Fry over a high heat for 2 minutes until the whites are golden brown around the edges and the yolks are golden and runny.

Remove the chilaquiles from the oven and top with the fried eggs, jalapeño cream, lime wedges and plenty of fresh coriander.

roasted aubergines with puy lentils & smoked mayo

INGREDIENTS

200g Puy lentils, thoroughly
  rinsed
1 celery stick
Whole bulb of garlic
1–2 rosemary sprigs
1 bay leaf
4 aubergines
A bunch of basil leaves,
  roughly chopped
A bunch of mint leaves,
  roughly chopped
100g sun-dried tomatoes,
  roughly chopped
3–4 tablespoons good-
  quality olive oil
Juice of 1 lemon
Sea salt and freshly ground
  black pepper

FOR THE MAYONNAISE

2 medium egg yolks
2 tablespoons lemon juice
200ml good-quality
  vegetable oil
1 teaspoon smoked paprika

This is a dramatic dish made using a tried-and-tested technique to cook the aubergines. They are simply grilled until buttery soft, unceremoniously split open and filled with olive oil and lemon. The lentils cook while the aubergines grill, then both are served alongside a sweet smoked mayo.

PREP TIME 30 MINUTES ✳ **COOK TIME 40 MINUTES** ✳ **SERVES 4**

Put the lentils in a saucepan and cover generously with cold water. Add the celery stick, garlic bulb, rosemary and bay leaf and simmer, uncovered, for about 25 minutes. Check the lentils at this point, but expect to continue cooking for a further 10–15 minutes – the lentils should be soft but not lacking bite. Drain and tip into a bowl. Disgard the celery stick, garlic bulb, rosemary and bay leaf – they have done their job.

Meanwhile, preheat the oven to its hottest setting. When it is roasting hot, turn it to the grill setting. Pierce the aubergines twice with a small, sharp knife to prevent them exploding under the grill. Place them on a baking sheet under the grill, with the oven door closed, for 20 minutes, turning half-way through, or until the skin is black and the flesh collapsed and soft. Remove from the oven and set aside.

Next make the mayonnaise. Put the egg yolks and lemon juice in a clean medium bowl and beat together using an electric whisk. Very slowly add the oil, constantly beating as you do so. The mixture will become thick and creamy. Stir through the smoked paprika and season to taste. Set aside.

Stir half the herbs through the lentils with the sun-dried tomatoes and 3 tablespoons of oil. Season to taste and set aside.

Slice the hot aubergines down their centre, being mindful not to cut all the way through and split them open. Drizzle each with the remaining oil, the lemon juice and remaining herbs. Season with black pepper and a pinch of salt.

Transfer the lentils to a large platter and arrange the aubergines on top or alongside. Serve each portion with a dollop of homemade smoked mayonnaise.

hasselback potatoes with creamy puy lentils & bacon

INGREDIENTS

150g Puy lentils, rinsed
   thoroughly
1kg large floury potatoes
40g unsalted butter
2 tablespoons olive oil
1 onion, finely chopped
8 garlic cloves, sliced
125g bacon lardons
125ml hot chicken stock
200ml double cream
Thyme leaves
Salt and freshly ground
   black pepper

One of the great ingredient marriages is Puy lentils and salty bacon and I've exploited this relationship a little further with the addition of crispy hasselback potatoes and cream. Hasselbacks are Swedish-style roasties, cooked like baked potatoes. This is a fabulous centrepiece that requires little skill, just a hot oven and an occasion.

PREP TIME 40 MINUTES ✳ **COOK TIME 1 HOUR 30 MINUTES** ✳ **SERVES 6**

Preheat the oven to 200°C/180°C fan/gas mark 6.

Put the lentils in a saucepan and cover generously with cold water. Simmer for 20–25 minutes over a medium–low heat until just soft – you still want a little 'bite' to them. Drain and set aside.

Meanwhile, prepare the potatoes. Starting at one end, slice the potatoes as thinly as possible, top to bottom, but without cutting right the way through. (A good tip here is to place a skewer on either side of the potato and slice down onto them; the skewers prevent the knife from cutting all the way through the potato – you don't want separate slices here.)

Melt the butter and 1 tablespoon of oil in a small saucepan. Place the potatoes in an ovenproof dish and brush them with the butter mixture, aiming to get some inside the potato slices. Transfer to the oven and roast for 30 minutes.

Meanwhile, heat the remaining tablespoon of oil in a large frying pan over a medium heat. Fry the onion and garlic until softened. Remove the mixture from the pan and set aside while you fry the lardons. Once the lardons are crisp, return the onion to the pan, along with the cooked lentils. Pour in the stock and cream and simmer for 5–8 minutes. Taste at this point and adjust the seasoning.

Remove the potatoes from the oven and spoon the creamy lentil mixture around them. Nestle a few thyme leaves into the lentils and give the dish a good grinding of black pepper. Return to the oven and roast for a further 30–35 minutes. Serve immediately.

salted caramel brownie mud cake

FOR THE BASE

250g dark chocolate
　digestive biscuits
85g lightly salted butter,
　melted

FOR THE FILLING

100g unsalted butter
100g dark chocolate
　(minimum 70% cocoa solids)
400g can black beans,
　drained and rinsed
2 large free-range eggs
160g golden caster sugar
1 tablespoon treacle
70g plain flour
50g cocoa powder
1 teaspoon vanilla bean paste

FOR THE SALTED CARAMEL

130g granulated sugar
20g unsalted butter
4 tablespoons double cream
2–3 drops vanilla extract
Pinch of sea salt flakes
3 tablespoons edible bronze
　or metallic sprinkles,
　to decorate

You will also need a 24cm,
　springform cake tin

The base of this mud cake is essentially dark chocolate biscuits, bashed and melded with butter, topped with a deep, dark brownie filling. The salted caramel is a frivolous extra, but one that your family and friends will surely appreciate. Do let the caramel cool completely, preferably overnight – it solidifies and sinks into the layer below, making this cake all the more delicious.

PREP TIME 45 MINUTES ✳ COOK TIME 35 MINUTES ✳ SERVES 8–10

Preheat the oven to 180°C/160°C fan/gas mark 4.

First make the base. Blitz the biscuits in a food processor to a fine crumb. Add the butter and blitz again until combined. Spoon the filling into a 24cm springform cake tin and press into the base using the back of an oiled spoon to ensure the crumbs are well compacted. Bake for 10 minutes, then set aside.

To make the filling, bring a medium saucepan of water to a simmer over a medium heat. Put the chocolate and butter into a bowl and set on the pan so that it is suspended over, but not touching, the simmering water. Melt gently, stirring occasionally. Set aside to cool slightly.

Put the beans into the bowl of a food processor and blitz to a rough paste. Add the eggs and sugar and continue to blend together. Add the cooled, melted chocolate and butter mixture, the treacle, flour, cocoa powder and vanilla. Blend until you have a thick, luxurious paste. Pour the brownie mixture over the cooled base and bake for 25 minutes. Remove from the oven and allow to cool completely in the tin.

Meanwhile, make the caramel. Put the sugar and 6 tablespoons cold water in a medium saucepan and allow to dissolve over a medium heat, then increase the heat and gently boil. Do not stir it at any stage but swirl the pan lightly (this will help prevent the caramel from crystallising on the sides). Once the caramel is a deep golden brown, remove from the heat and swirl in the butter. Working quickly, beat in the cream with a whisk. Stir through the vanilla paste and sea salt flakes. With the brownie still in its tin, pour the caramel over the cooled chocolate filling and allow to set for an afternoon or overnight in a cool spot. Rain the edible bronze over the cake and serve in slices.

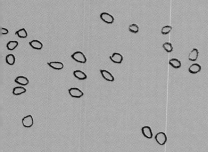

green

PEAS

✳

BROAD BEANS

✳

RUNNER BEANS

✳

FLAGEOLET BEANS

✳

EDAMAME BEANS

✳

MUNG BEANS

✳

GREEN LENTILS

✳

GREEN SPLIT PEAS

pea, potato & saffron strudel

INGREDIENTS

2 tablespoons olive oil
1 small onion, finely
   chopped
½ small fennel bulb,
   finely sliced
2 large garlic cloves, crushed
2 medium floury potatoes,
   peeled and cut into
   2–3cm cubes
Small pinch of saffron
   strands
250ml hot vegetable stock
200g peas
Zest and juice of 1 large
   unwaxed lemon
½ bunch of dill, fronds
   finely chopped, plus a few
   to garnish
60g unsalted butter, melted
6 sheets of filo pastry
50g Cheddar, grated
Salt and freshly ground
   black pepper

Feather-light, layered filo pasty encases a heavier, soft, savoury filling in my version of the infamous strudel. In my opinion, saffron is a must, offering a distinctive flavour amongst the well-heeled potato, shallot and pea element. Be confident when wrapping the strudel – swift, brave movements will often prevent the filo tearing and the filling escaping.

PREP TIME 35 MINUTES ✳ **COOK TIME 1 HOUR** ✳ **SERVES 6**

Heat the oil in a large, heavy-based frying pan. Add the onion and fennel with a pinch of salt and sauté over a medium heat, stirring frequently until they are golden, soft and sticky. Add the garlic, cook for 1 minute until you can smell the garlic aroma before stirring in the potatoes and saffron.

Pour the steaming stock over the potato mixture and cook, covered with a lid, sitting askew, for 20–25 minutes, or until the potatoes are soft when poked with a knife. Increase the heat for a few minutes to boil off any remaining liquid: you want the filling to be slightly juicy but not to soak through the pastry.

Remove the pan from the heat and stir in the frozen peas, lemon zest and juice and 2 tablespoons of chopped dill. The peas will cook in the residual heat of the pan. Allow the filling to cool completely before using.

Preheat the oven to 180°C/160°C fan/gas mark 4. Brush a large baking sheet with melted butter and lay a filo sheet ontop. Repeat with all six sheets, placing them on top of one another, brushing them generously with butter each time.

Spoon half the filling lengthways along the middle of the pastry sheet. Sprinkle over the cheese and top with the remaining filling. Roll up into a parcel, keeping the seam underneath. Tuck the ends in as you roll. Brush the whole strudel with a little more butter, top with a few remaining fronds of dill and bake for 20–25 minutes, or until the top is crusty and golden brown. Check the strudel after the first 10 minutes and gauge whether the heat needs reducing slightly; the pastry shouldn't be brown at this stage.

Remove from the oven and allow your strudel to sit for 5-10 miniutes before serving in stout slices.

goat's cheese, lemon & pea ravioli with pink peppercorns

FOR THE PASTA

200g '00' flour, plus extra
   for dusting
2 large eggs
1 scant teaspoon olive oil

FOR THE FILLING

100g frozen peas
125g soft goat's cheese
1 medium egg yolk
15g Parmesan, grated
Zest of 1 unwaxed lemon
20g butter
1 teaspoon pink
peppercorns, crushed
½ tablespoon chopped
   dill fronds
Salt and freshly ground
   black pepper

Ravioli is to a romantic dinner what a 'little black dress' is to an Italian wardrobe: simple, stylish and so pretty. This isn't one to rush, instead the process of making the pasta should be enjoyed almost as much as eating the finished dish. One tip: make sure the seams are well secured, there is nothing more disappointing than seeing ravioli filling disappear into a simmering pot.

PREP TIME 1 HOUR ✳ COOK TIME 10 MINUTES ✳ SERVES 2

First make the pasta. Put the flour, eggs and olive oil in the bowl of a food processor and blitz to create a fine crumb with no flecks of flour remaining. Form into a dough using your hands and knead firmly until the dough is no longer sticky and is elastic to the touch. Wrap in clingfilm and allow to rest in the fridge for at least 30 minutes.

Meanwhile, prepare the filling. Bring a medium saucepan of salted water to the boil, add the peas and cook for 3–5 minutes. Strain and tip into a small bowl. Lightly crush the peas with a fork before mixing with the goat's cheese, egg yolk, Parmesan and lemon zest. Season to taste.

Once rested, roll the pasta out using a pasta machine. Start at the widest setting and work your way down to the second to last setting to create two long, thin sheets of pasta. Transfer to a floured work surface and use a medium round cutter to stamp out 20 rounds from the pasta. Place a spoonful of filling in the centre of 10 of the discs. Brush a little water around the edge, then place the reserved discs on top. Press down firmly around the edge of each raviolo to seal in the filling and set aside for at least 10 minutes.

Melt the butter in a medium saucepan on a low-medium heat. Cook until foaming and beginning to lightly brown. It should have a biscuit-like smell. Remove from the heat.

Bring a large saucepan of water to the boil. Salt generously, then lower in the ravioli, stirring briefly to stop them sticking together. Cook for 3 minutes, then drain and gently combine with the browned butter. Divide between two bowls and sprinkle with the peppercorns and dill. Serve immediately.

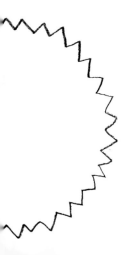

Asian-spiced roast chicken, pea & wasabi purée & pickled carrots

INGREDIENTS

1 medium free-range
  chicken, legs trussed
2 limes, halved
1 garlic bulb, halved
  horizontally
1 red chilli, finely chopped
1 lemongrass stalk, inner
  removed and chopped
2 star anise
3 cloves
1 teaspoon cumin
1 teaspoon ground ginger
3 black peppercorns
3 tablespoons sunflower or
  vegetable oil
Salt and freshly ground
  black pepper

Handful of alfalfa sprouts,
  to serve

FOR THE PICKLED CARROTS

3 carrots, peeled
70ml rice wine vinegar
1 tablespoon caster sugar
½ teaspoon coriander seeds
½ teaspoon mustard seeds

FOR THE PEA PURÉE

600g frozen peas
3 tablespoons cold milk
3 teaspoons wasabi paste

The roast chicken – so iconic, so reliable and comforting, but often very predictable. This version has been jazzed up a little and enjoys the company of Asian spices, an insanely beautiful wasabi purée and quick-pickled carrots.

PREP TIME 40 MINUTES ✳ **COOK TIME 1½ HOURS** ✳ **SERVES 5–6**

Preheat the oven to 200°C/180°C fan/gas mark 6.

Put the chicken in a large roasting tin. Place one halved lime into the cavity of the chicken and the remaining halves into the roasting tin around the bird, along with the garlic. Blitz the chilli and lemongrass together in the bowl of a food processor and set aside. Pound the star anise, cloves, cumin, ginger and peppercorns together using a spice or coffee grinder or a pestle and mortar until you have a powder. Combine the spices and chilli mixture together and rub generously over the skin of the chicken. Drizzle with the oil, season to taste and roast in the middle of the oven for an hour, by which time the skin should be golden brown and the juices should run clear when the thickest part of the chicken flesh is pierced with a skewer. Rest for 10 minutes.

Meanwhile, use a peeler to cut thin ribbons from the carrots. Heat the vinegar, sugar and 125ml of water in a small saucepan. Allow the sugar to dissolve and bring to a gentle simmer. Remove from the heat and add the coriander and mustard seeds. Put the carrots in a small bowl or sterilised jar. Pour over the pickling liquid, turning the carrot ribbons so they are covered, and leave to cool and pickle for at least 30 minutes – longer if you can.

For the purée, bring a medium saucepan of salted water to the boil and add the peas. Reduce the heat to a simmer and cook for 10 minutes. Strain and blend to make a smooth purée. Adjust the consistency by adding the milk gradually until the purée is of a slightly loose, dropping consistency. Stir through the wasabi and season to taste. Keep warm.

Drain the carrots and arrange on a plate with the purée and roast chicken. Serve sprinkled with the alfalfa sprouts.

spinach, pea & mint green eggs & ham

INGREDIENTS

300g frozen peas
2 tablespoons olive oil
3 large banana shallots,
   quartered
2 garlic cloves, crushed
150g young leaf spinach
Pinch of ground nutmeg
140ml double cream
4 tablespoons chopped
   flat-leaf parsley
4 tablespoons chopped mint
4 eggs
3 large slices of ham, torn
Salt and freshly ground
   black pepper

When a recipe comes together with little effort or forethought, when it appeals to adults and children alike and when all that's needed is a frying pan, you can be sure it's a good 'un. Remove from the heat just as the yolk of the eggs are still runny and present with warmed bread, ready to dunk.

PREP TIME 10 MINUTES ✳ COOK TIME 25 MINUTES ✳ SERVES 4

Bring a medium saucepan of water to the boil, add the peas and cook for just 3 minutes, not a minute longer. Drain and set aside.

Heat the oil in a large heavy-based frying pan over a medium heat. Add the shallots and cook for 4–6 minutes, allowing them to colour lightly. Add the garlic and cook for a further minute.

Add the peas to the pan and crush lightly with the back of a spoon. Add the spinach, cover the pan for 2 minutes or until the spinach is wilted (if your pan doesn't have a lid, improvise with a baking tray). Add the nutmeg, cream and half the herbs. Simmer this luscious mixture for 3 minutes, stirring occasionally. Season to taste.

Reduce the heat, make four wells in the spinach and pea mixture and crack an egg into each well. Nestle the ham into the pan. Cover the pan and cook for 10–12 minutes, or until the egg whites are just set. Sprinkle over the remaining herbs. Serve with crusty sourdough.

broad bean, ham hock
& wholegrain mustard pie

INGREDIENTS
2 ham hocks
2 bay leaves
1 teaspoon black
    peppercorns
220g broad beans (podded
    weight)
1½ tablespoons wholegrain
    mustard
150ml crème fraîche
1 teaspoon coriander seeds,
    crushed
4 tablespoons finely
    chopped cornichons
1 tablespoon plain flour
½ small bunch of flat-leaf
    parsley, chopped
300ml cider
1 medium egg, beaten
Salt and freshly ground
    black pepper

FOR THE PASTRY
175g plain flour
Tiny pinch of salt
150g butter, diced
90ml soured cream
1 tablespoon poppy seeds

You will also need a 26cm
    pie dish

A thrifty ham hock is the backbone to this recipe and, partnered with tangy cornichons and cream, it equates to pie heaven. The reassuring creamy filling is encased in fudgy pastry, highly glazed and sprinkled with poppy seeds.

PREP TIME 40 MINUTES + 1 HOUR CHILLING ✳ COOK TIME 4 HOURS ✳ SERVES 6

Place the ham hocks, bay leaves and peppercorns in a large saucepan. Cover generously with cold water and bring to a simmer. Cover and cook for 3 hours until tender. Keep your eye on the water and top up every so often, as needed. Once the ham hocks are cooked, remove them from the pan. Separate the meat from the bone – I find it easiest to use my hands. Pull away large chunks of the meat and roughly chop. You'll need about 500g of cooked ham hock.

Bring a separate saucepan of salted water to the boil. Add the beans and simmer for 5–6 minutes until just tender. Drain and set aside.

For the pastry, put the flour, salt and butter in a food processor and pulse until fully incorporated. Alternatively, rub the butter into the flour in a large bowl using your fingertips. Add the soured cream and pulse for 2–3 seconds or stir by hand. Shape into a ball, wrap in clingfilm and chill for 30 minutes.

Select an enormous bowl and combine the ham, broad beans, mustard, crème fraîche, coriander seeds, cornichons, flour and parsley. Pour the cider into a small saucepan over a medium heat and allow to reduce by half. Cool slightly then add to the ham hock mixture. Season to taste.

Empty the filling into a 26cm pie dish and brush the edge of the dish with a little beaten egg. Roll out the pastry to the thickness of a £1 coin and place over the filling. Crimp the edges of the pastry to secure it to the edge of the dish, brush the surface with more beaten egg and chill for 30 minutes.

Meanwhile, preheat the oven to 180°C/160°C fan/gas mark 4. Remove the pie from the fridge, glaze with egg and scatter with poppy seeds. Bake on the middle shelf of the oven for 30–35 minutes until the pastry is golden and you can just see the filling bubbling. Allow to sit for a few minutes before serving.

*TIP
You can also use
200g dried broad beans
(fava beans), soaked
overnight. Simply place
the broad beans in a large
saucepan of salted water
and bring to the boil over
a high heat, then lower
the heat to a simmer and
cook for 25–30 minutes
or until the broad beans
are al dente.

crispy pancetta
& broad bean spaghetti

INGREDIENTS
250g fresh broad beans,
   unpodded
8 thin slices of pancetta
400g dried spaghetti
70g Parmesan, grated
4 egg yolks, lightly whisked
Zest of 1 unwaxed lemon
2 tablespoons chopped
   flat-leaf parsley
Olive oil, for drizzling
   (optional)
Sea salt and freshly ground
   black pepper

All too often the time for dinner arrives and the fridge is unprepared, though this technique of an enriched pasta sauce is a useful trick to have in these moments. Pasta is a given in my storecupboard and generally there is a box of eggs sitting in wait. Simply mix egg yolks, finely grated hard cheese and pasta water, stir into your recipe and add the 'bits'. This combination of sweet young beans with summer herbs and salty pancetta fits perfectly.

PREP TIME 25 MINUTES ✳ **COOK TIME 10 MINUTES** ✳ **SERVES 4**

Bring a medium saucepan of salted water to the boil. Add the broad beans and cook for 3 minutes. Strain, slit the pods and use your thumb to push out the beans. Pop the bright green beans from their grey skins. This double podding might seem a little laborious but will certainly improve both the look and taste of the final dish. Set aside.

Place a frying pan over a medium–high heat and fry the pancetta for 4–5 minutes until browned and crispy – you shouldn't need oil; the fat in the pancetta should suffice. Once cooked, lay the slices on kitchen paper to remove any excess oil. Break into small shards.

Bring a large saucepan of salted water to a rolling boil and slide the spaghetti into the pan. Reduce the heat a touch and cook for 7 minutes, or until the pasta is al dente. Drain, reserving some of the cooking water. Return the spaghetti to the pan along with a ladleful of the cooking water, the Parmesan, egg yolks and lemon zest. Toss everything together until the cooking water, cheese and yolks start to emulsify into a sauce that gently coats the pasta. If there isn't enough sauce add another half-ladleful of cooking water. Toss through the broad beans, half the pancetta and the parsley. Season well with salt.

Divide the pasta between warmed bowls, top with the remaining pancetta and a drizzle of oil, if desired. Serve immediately.

smoked trout, broad beans & freekeh salad

INGREDIENTS
200g wholegrain freekeh
4 garlic cloves, halved
150g broad beans (podded
  weight)
1 celery stick, finely sliced
75g walnuts, toasted and
  chopped (reserve a few
  whole ones for garnish)
½ bunch of curly parsley,
  finely chopped
2 small smoked trout fillets,
  flaked into large pieces
Salt and freshly ground
  black pepper

FOR THE DRESSING
2 small garlic cloves,
  crushed
3 tablespoons olive oil

Juice of ½ lemon
1 tablespoon runny honey
1 tablespoon cider vinegar

It feels like I've spent much of my thirties pregnant and with each baby I am more conscious of the fuel required to stay energised. This salad is perfection for me, as I trust the essential oils of smoked fish and the slow-realising energy of the freekeh. Sweet broad beans and a somewhat tart dressing pull the salad together.

PREP TIME 20 MINUTES ✳ **COOK TIME 25 MINUTES** ✳ **SERVES 4–6**

Bring a medium saucepan of water to the boil and add the freekeh and garlic. Bring back to the boil, then cover the pan and reduce the heat to low. Simmer for 15–20 minutes, or until the grains are al dente and the cloves are soft. Drain the freekeh, discard the garlic and set aside.

Meanwhile, bring a small saucepan of salted water to a rolling boil and add the broad beans. Cook for 3–4 minutes, then drain and plunge into iced water. Allow to cool a little before popping the bright green beans from their grey skins.

To make the dressing, whisk all the ingredients together, or put in a jam jar with a tight-fitting lid and shake vigorously. Taste and adjust according to your palate.

Tip the warm freekeh into a very large mixing bowl with the beans, celery, walnuts and parsley and gently toss together. Add the flaked trout to the salad and season with salt and black pepper. Tip into a serving bowl and spoon over the dressing. Sprinkle with the reserved walnuts and serve.

✳TIP
The cooked grain keeps for well over a week in the fridge, so I'll often cook more than I need for a particular recipe just so I have extra on hand to stir into soups or salads during the week.

Portuguese deep-fried runner beans

INGREDIENTS

500g runner beans, trimmed
and stringed
2 litres flavourless vegetable
oil (such as sunflower),
for deep-frying

FOR THE BATTER

100g plain flour
1 teaspoon salt
2 eggs, lightly beaten

FOR THE YOGURT DIP

2 teaspoons coriander seeds
100ml plain yogurt
Zest and juice of
½ unwaxed lemon
1 tablespoon finely chopped
dill fronds
1 tablespoon finely chopped
flat-leaf parsley
Salt and freshly ground
black pepper

A centuries-old recipe, known in Portuguese as Peixinhos da Horta, which literally means 'vegetable garden fishies', as the finished beans resemble small pieces of colourful fish. Serve with a heavily herbed yogurt for an unassuming and effective appetiser.

PREP TIME 20 MINUTES ✳ COOK TIME 15 MINUTES ✳ SERVES 3–4 AS A SIDE

First make the batter. Tip the flour and salt into a large mixing bowl. Add 175ml of cold water slowly into the flour, mixing as you go, followed by the eggs. Beat using a wooden spoon or whisk until the mixture is fairly smooth – not to worry if there is a lump or two – but take care not to over-mix. Set the batter aside to rest.

To make the dip, toast the coriander seeds in a dry frying pan, then tip them into a small, robust bowl. Use the end of a rolling pin to bash the spices before adding the yogurt, lemon zest and juice and chopped herbs. Season lightly and set aside.

Bring a large saucepan of salted water to the boil. Drop the runner beans into the water and boil for 4 minutes. Drain through a colander, then refresh under cold running water to stop the cooking process. Pat dry with kitchen paper and set aside.

Pour in enough oil to fill a heavy-bottomed pan to a depth of about 6cm and set over a medium–high heat. To test whether the oil is hot, drop a small cube of bread into it: if it sizzles immediately, the oil is ready. Dip the beans into the batter, one at a time, and carefully lower them into the hot oil batter. Work in batches so as not to overcrowd the pan. Once the beans are lightly golden in colour, use a slotted spoon to remove them from the oil and drain on kitchen paper. Repeat with the remaining beans, discarding any leftover batter. Serve the hot beans in a pile with the dip alongside.

salmon, hazelnut & runner bean salad

INGREDIENTS
Olive oil, for greasing
4 x 200g plump salmon
    fillets, skin on
400g runner beans, topped
    and tailed
½ small bunch of mint,
    leaves roughly chopped
3 tablespoons dill fronds
100g hazelnuts, skin on,
    roughly chopped
150g ricotta cheese
Salt and freshly ground
    black pepper

FOR THE DRESSING
2 tablespoons olive oil
1 tablespoon cider vinegar
Zest of 1 unwaxed lemon
    and juice of ½
1 teaspoon Dijon mustard

We ate this salmon at Easter; I felt like a change from a usual roast lunch and this pretty, light recipe seemed to fit. It is uncomplicated – the salmon is baked with lemon and seasoning and served atop blanched beans. Be sure to make the dressing as tart as you like it as the sour note complements the soft ricotta.

PREP TIME 15 MINUTES ✳ COOK TIME 25–30 MINUTES ✳ SERVES 4

Preheat the oven to 200°C/180°C fan/gas mark 6. Brush a little oil over the base of an ovenproof dish large enough to accommodate the salmon fillets, and lay your fish inside. Season the fillets well and roast for 18–20 minutes. The timing will depend on the thickness of your fillets, but be vigilant not to overcook the salmon.

Meanwhile, make the dressing by combining the oil, cider vinegar, lemon zest and juice, and mustard in a jar. Seal tightly with a lid and shake until well combined.

Bring a large saucepan of water to a constant, steamy simmer. Slice the beans on the diagonal, about 2–3cm in length. Drop the beans into the simmering water and cook for about 7 minutes until they are tender but retain a little bite. Drain and refresh under cold running water to stop the cooking process. Tip into a bowl and pour over the dressing and herbs. Mix well.

Fry the hazelnuts in a dry frying pan over a medium–high heat until just toasted.

Spoon the dressed runner beans onto a large platter and dot with spoonfuls of ricotta. Top with the salmon and scatter over the toasted hazelnuts.

smoked cheddar, chive & runner bean frittata

INGREDIENTS

350g new potatoes, scrubbed
200g runner beans, cut into
  2–3cm slices
8 large free-range eggs
2 tablespoons finely
  chopped chives
3 tablespoons finely
  chopped flat-leaf parsley
2 tablespoons finely
  chopped basil
A glug of olive oil
100g smoked Cheddar,
  grated

I always think of the frittata as a sturdy omelette – a recipe that can withstand being cooked the day before, wrapped and lugged around in a picnic hamper. As with many egg recipes, the flavour really comes from the added ingredients, so do buy additions that pack a punch. My tip is a smoked cheese, as the flavour flatters the eggs.

PREP TIME 10 MINUTES ✳ COOK TIME 40-45 MINUTES ✳ SERVES 4–6

Bring a large pan of salted water to the boil over a medium–high heat. Add the potatoes and cook for 15 minutes, uncovered, before adding the beans to the pan and simmering for a further 5-6 minutes. Drain and set aside. As soon as the potatoes are cool enough to handle, slice them into thick coins.

Whisk together the eggs and half the herbs in a large bowl. Preheat the grill to medium–high.

Heat the olive oil in a large, heavy-based frying pan and add the potatoes. Cook over a medium–high heat for 10–15 minutes until the slices are golden. Add the beans and gently combine the two. Pour over the egg mixture. Sprinkle over the cheese and the remaining chives. Cook over a low heat for 10–14 minutes, then transfer to the grill for the final 10–15 minutes to ensure the centre is cooked through and the top is slightly golden.

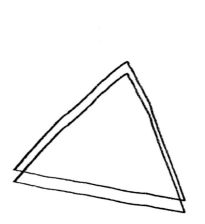
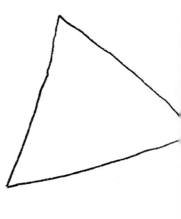

cheesy cauliflower
& flageolet with truffle oil

INGREDIENTS

1 large cauliflower, leaves
  removed and stalk trimmed
1–2 tablespoons extra virgin
  truffle oil
40g unsalted butter
40g plain flour
Pinch of mustard powder
Pinch of cayenne pepper
350ml whole milk
400g can flageolet beans,
  drained and rinsed
2 tablespoons roughly
  chopped flat-leaf parsley
75g mature Cheddar, grated
Salt and freshly ground
  black pepper

Very little truffle oil can create quite the impact. The classic cauliflower cheese has been embellished with a pool of soft beans and just a touch of truffle. A stunning family centerpiece, ideal for a bracing winter's day.

PREP TIME 20 MINUTES ✳ **COOK TIME 45 MINUTES**
✳ **SERVES 4 OR 6 AS A SIDE**

Preheat the oven to 180°C/160°C fan/gas mark 4.

Bring a large saucepan of salted water to the boil and place the whole cauliflower in the water. Simmer for 15 minutes, turning half-way through, before removing from the water. Place in an ovenproof serving dish. While the cauliflower is still hot, drizzle over the truffle oil and leave to infuse.

Meanwhile, make the cheese sauce. Melt the butter in a small saucepan over a medium heat, then stir in the flour, mustard powder and cayenne and mix to a roux. Continue to cook for 2 minutes, then gradually whisk in the milk. Keep stirring over a low heat until the sauce thickens. Season to taste with salt and black pepper.

Remove the sauce from the heat and gently stir in the beans, parsley and half the cheese. Check the seasoning.

Pour the cheese sauce over the top of the cauliflower, allowing the beans to puddle at the base of the dish. Scatter the remaining cheese over the top of the cauliflower. Bake in the centre of the oven for 25–30 minutes until bubbly and golden brown.

flageolet beans with baked ricotta & asparagus

INGREDIENTS
Large knob of butter
1 tablespoon olive oil
3 shallots, sliced
3 garlic cloves, sliced
1 small green chilli,
   deseeded and finely
   chopped
100ml white wine
400g can flageolet beans,
   drained and rinsed
Small handful of flat-leaf
   parsley, roughly chopped
80g asparagus tips
250g ricotta cheese
1 medium egg, lightly beaten
100g cherry tomatoes,
   halved

TO SERVE
A grating of Parmesan
A drizzle of olive oil

A lovely simple recipe to have up your sleeve that requires no more than ten minutes worth of preparation. Use as an accompliment to a leafy salad or bulk out with a smoky fish and eat for supper.

PREP TIME 10 MINUTES ✳ **COOK TIME 30 MINUTES** ✳ **SERVES 4**

Preheat the oven to 180°C/160°C fan/gas mark 4.

Heat the butter and oil in a large frying pan over a medium heat. Add the shallots and garlic to the pan. Gently soften for a few minutes before adding the green chilli. Continue to cook until everything is soft and the shallots are almost translucent. Pour in the white wine and cook until reduced by half before tipping in the flageolet beans. Add the parsley. Give everything a good stir so all the ingredients are well distributed.

Meanwhile, bring a small saucepan of water to the boil and add the asparagus tips. Blanch for 3–4 minutes until just soft, then drain and immediately run under cold water to stop the cooking process. Add the asparagus to the beans.

Gently combine the ricotta and beaten egg in a small bowl to form a thick paste. Tip the asparagus and bean mixture into an ovenproof dish and dot over the ricotta mixture, leaving spaces where the vegetables are visable. Dot the cherry tomatoes over the surface, transfer to the hot oven and bake for 25 minutes. Remove from the oven and serve with a grating a fresh Parmesan and a drizzle of olive oil.

flageolet & artichoke dip with toasted spices

INGREDIENTS

400g can flageolet beans,
  drained and rinsed
390g can artichoke hearts,
  drained
1 garlic clove
Juice of 1 lemon
3 tablespoons olive oil
1 teaspoon coriander seeds
1 teaspoon cumin seeds
1 teaspoon garam masala
Salt and freshly ground
  black pepper

Toasted pitta bread, to serve

A shallow, warm bowl of this purée sits wonderfully alongside a roasted leg of lamb. Think of it as another side. I see no reason why you couldn't swap the flageolet beans to butter beans or any other soft, white beans.

PREP TIME 10 MINUTES ✳ COOK TIME 5 MINUTES ✳ SERVES 6–8

Put the flageolet beans, artichoke hearts, garlic and lemon juice into the bowl of a food processor and whizz until just smooth, adding a little more lemon juice if necessary. Decant into a bowl and season to taste.

Heat a touch of the oil in a frying pan over a high heat. Add the spices and fry to release their aroma – this should take no longer than 1–2 minutes. Remove from the heat and stir through the remaining oil.

Make a generous indentation in the dip and pour in the hot spices and oil. Serve with toasted pitta bread for scooping up the dip.

edamame, quinoa, avocado & roasted tomato salad

INGREDIENTS

300g cherry tomatoes,
  multi-coloured if possible
2 tablespoons olive oil
250g quinoa
150g edamame beans, fresh
  or frozen
1 ripe avocado, halved,
  stoned, peeled and sliced
2 tablespoons finely
  chopped dill fronds
½ teaspoon sea salt
1 teaspoon poppy seeds
Salt and freshly ground
  black pepper

Roasting cherry tomatoes seems to be luxurious. The already sweet, tiny red orbs become even sweeter in a hot oven and seem to collapse dramatically in the heat. Their juices create the beginnings of a dressing for the quinoa, enhanced by the olive oil.

PREP TIME 15 MINUTES ✳ **COOK TIME 20 MINUTES** ✳ **SERVES 4**

Preheat the oven to 180°C/160°C fan/gas mark 4. Spread the tomatoes on a baking tray and drizzle with oil. Season and roast for 8–10 minutes until the skins have blistered.

Meanwhile, cook the quinoa. Bring 500ml salted water to the boil, tip in the quinoa and cook for about 12 minutes, adding the edamame beans halfway through cooking. Drain and transfer to a large mixing bowl. Working gently and using a large metal spoon, stir through most of the hot tomatoes (leaving a few to scatter on top). Add the avocado and dill. Scrunch over the salt.

Serve the warm salad on a platter or in a large bowl scattered with the reserved tomatoes and poppy seeds.

Vietnamese meatballs & edamame broth

FOR THE MEATBALLS
500g pork mince
Thumb-sized piece of
  ginger, peeled and grated
2 garlic cloves, crushed
½ tablespoon fish sauce
1 tablespoon runny honey
½ red chilli, finely chopped
1 tablespoon sesame oil
5 tablespoons plum sauce
Salt and freshly ground
  black pepper

FOR THE BROTH
2 litres chicken stock
1½ tablespoons fish sauce
5 kaffir lime leaves
1 lemongrass stalk, bashed
1 cinnamon stick
½ whole red chilli
150g vermicelli rice noodles
170g frozen edamame beans

TO GARNISH
Small bunch of Thai basil
Small bunch of mint
8 mixed radishes, finely
  sliced
½ red chilli, sliced
1 tablespoon black sesame
  seeds (optional)

Lime wedges, to serve

These simple meatballs, made with pork mince, are rolled in sweet plum sauce and served atop a plethora of fresh vegetables and slithery rice noodles. Eat – no, slurp – from bowls like no one is listening and enjoy the fresh, vivid flavour.

PREP TIME 40 MINUTES ✳ **COOK TIME 40 MINUTES** ✳ **SERVES 4**

First make the meatballs. Put the mince in a large bowl and break it up using your hands. Add the ginger and garlic followed by the fish sauce, honey and chilli. Season with salt and black pepper and mix well until everything is combined. Divide the mixture into 12 even-sized balls and chill until needed.

Next, prepare the broth. Put the stock, fish sauce, lime leaves, lemongrass, cinnamon and chilli in a large saucepan over a medium heat. Bring to the boil, then reduce the heat to a simmer and cook for 20 minutes. Discard the lime leaves, lemongrass, cinnamon, and chilli. Turn up the heat, add the vermicelli and beans to the pan and cook for 7 minutes. Keep warm until ready to serve.

Heat the sesame oil in a large, heavy-based frying pan over a medium heat. Brown the meatballs, rolling them occasionally so that they colour evenly. Cover the pan and leave over a moderate heat until cooked right through – a good 10 minutes. Meanwhile, gently heat the plum sauce in a small saucepan for 3 minutes, or until it becomes thick and syrupy. Drain the meatballs on kitchen paper, dabbing off any excess oil. Toss the meatballs and plum sauce together in a tray until the meatballs are well coated and sticky.

Using a pair of tongs, divide the noodles between four deep bowls, ladle over the broth and top with the meatballs. Garnish with the basil, mint, radishes, chilli and black sesame seeds. Season with a good squeeze of lime juice and serve.

*TIP
Rolling the limes across the worktop
makes it easier to extract all their juice.

lemon chicken
& green pea mash pie

INGREDIENTS

6 skinless, boneless chicken
   thighs
1 large garlic bulb, halved
   horizontally
1 unwaxed lemon, quartered
Bunch of spring onions,
   trimmed and cut into two
1 large courgette, halved
   lengthways amd cut into
   1cm crescents
2 tablespoons olive oil
100ml full-fat crème fraîche
100ml hot vegetable stock
15g mint, chopped
Salt and freshly ground
   black pepper

FOR THE MASH

500g white floury potatoes,
   peeled and cut into large
   chunks
200g frozen peas
2 tablespoons unsalted
   butter
1 garlic clove, chopped

TO GARNISH

1 tablespoon chopped
   flat-leaf parsley
1 teaspoon pink
   peppercorns, crushed

More often than we would hope, the months of April and May in the UK are tarnished with cold. Evenings require a warming meal to be eaten indoors. The filling for this pie is predominantly baked in the oven and then covered with a gentle pea and potato mash, before returning to the oven so it's easy on us cooks.

PREP TIME 40 MINUTES ✳ **COOK TIME 1 HOUR 25 MINUTES** ✳ **SERVES 6**

Preheat the oven to 200°C/180°C fan/gas mark 6.

Put the chicken, garlic, lemon, courgette and spring onions in a large roasting dish with the oil. Season well and roast until just golden, for 30–35 minutes, turning once halfway through. Remove from the oven and set aside to cool.

Meanwhile, prepare the mash. Put the potatoes in a large pan of water and bring to the boil. Simmer for about 20 minutes, or until tender. Add the peas and continue to cook for 4–5 minutes. Drain and mash to a rough, smashed texture. Stir through the butter and garlic, then season liberally with salt.

Once the chicken is cool enough to handle, shred into bite-sized pieces. Squeeze the garlic purée from the roasted bulb and any juice from the lemon and stir through the chicken and vegetable mixture. Stir in the crème fraîche, chicken stock and mint. Taste and season accordingly.

Assemble your pie by decanting the filling into a suitable ovenproof dish and dolloping the green mash over the top. At this point, the pie can be cooled completely and kept for 1–2 days in the fridge until needed.

When ready to cook, lower the oven to 180°C/160°C fan/gas mark 4. Cook the pie for 40–45 minutes, until the filling is piping hot. Just before serving, place under a hot grill for 5 minutes to brown the mash. Sprinkle with parsley and pink peppercorns, then serve.

✳TIP
Don't be tempted to use half-fat crème fraîche, it tends to split during cooking.

sprouting mung bean & crab salad

INGREDIENTS
100g sprouting mung beans
½ red chilli, deseeded and
   finely chopped
3 tablespoons finely
   chopped chives
1 spring onion, finely
   chopped
1 dressed crab

FOR THE DRESSING
2 tablespoons light olive oil
Zest and juice of 1 large lime
Thumb sized piece of ginger,
   peeled and finely grated
Drizzle of runny honey

Inner-city living doesn't give many opportunities to hone green-fingered skills, so learning to create a garden of sorts, amongst Kilner jars, has been an unexpected pleasure. Here, lavish crabmeat is eked out and tossed amongst fresh spouts and a hot, fiery dressing for an elegant salad.

PREP TIME 12 MINUTES ✳ SERVES 2–3

For the dressing, combine the oil, lime zest and juice, ginger and honey until combined. Set aside until needed.

In a large mixing bowl toss together the spouting mung beans, chilli, chives and spring onion. Using a gentle touch, add the crab meat and the dressing. Spoon onto plates and serve with bruschetta for a light lunch or starter.

chicken with mung beans, prosciutto & rosemary

INGREDIENTS

250g mung beans, soaked
  overnight and drained
4 rosemary sprigs, plus 1
  tablespoon chopped leaves
3 garlic cloves, bashed
4 tablespoons olive oil
Juice of 1 lemon
4–6 unskinned, boneless
  chicken thighs,
  or 4 chicken legs
6 banana shallots, halved
  lengthways
200ml hot vegetable stock
6 slices of prosciutto ham
Salt and freshly ground
  black pepper

This is one of those simple recipes that can be experimented with and developed at will. Other varieties of bean work well and a dash of cream would certainly enrich the dish. My only other tip is to cook the mung beans until they are 'the other side' of soft – that way they will soak up more cooking juices in the oven.

PREP TIME 20 MINUTES + OVERNIGHT SOAKING ✳ COOK TIME 1 HOUR
✳ SERVES 4

Cover the soaked mung beans abundantly with cold water, at least twice their volume. Add half the rosemary sprigs and the garlic to the pan and bring to a furious boil, then reduce the heat to a simmer, skimming occasionally, and cook more gently for 20–25 minutes. Once cooked, strain, discard the rosemary sprigs and stir through the garlic, 2 tablespoons of the oil and the lemon juice. Season to taste and keep warm.

Preheat the oven to 180°C/160°C fan/gas mark 4.

Season the skin of the chicken thighs. Heat the remaining oil in a large, heavy-based frying pan over a medium–high heat. Brown the chicken in batches, skin-side down, for 5–8 minutes, or until the skin is a deep golden brown. There is no need to fry the underside at this point – the chicken gets further cooking in the oven. Remove from the pan, add a touch more olive oil if needed and fry the shallot halves for 4–5 minutes over a high heat until soft and golden.

Empty the mung beans into a shallow ovenproof dish and nestle the shallots among them, along with the remaining rosemary sprigs. Pour over the stock. Add the chicken legs, pushing them down slightly into the beans. Season well and cook in the oven for 20–25 minutes.

Remove the dish from the oven and place the strips of prosciutto over the chicken and sprinkle with the chopped rosemary. Return the dish to the oven for a further 5 minutes until the prosciutto is crispy. Serve.

Thai coconut soup with edamame beans

INGREDIENTS

Small handful of coriander
2 lemongrass stalks
Thumb-sized piece of
  galangal (or use ginger if
  you can't find galangal)
4 kaffir lime leaves
1 garlic clove
1 red chilli, deseeded and
  halved
3 shallots, halved lengthways
1 tablespoon palm sugar
400ml can full-fat coconut
  milk
5–6 small or button
  mushrooms, sliced
100g frozen edamame beans
Juice of 4 limes
4 tablespoons fish sauce
Salt and freshly ground
  black pepper

TO GARNISH

Coriander leaves
Red chilli, deseeded and
  sliced thinly
Lime wedges
Kaffir lime leaves, thinly
  sliced

Steamed basmati rice,
  to serve

With the confidence of a teenager, somewhat oblivious and lacking insight, I travelled to Thailand solo for a holiday. Realising my fragility, my week was mostly spent in one place, head down, hoping to be ignored and slurping Thai coconut soups. This soup, or a similar version, became my mainstay. The base of this soup is a heavily infused coconut milk, which is the key, so keep tasting it to make sure you're happy. Serve with rice.

PREP TIME 25 MINUTES ✳ COOK TIME 20 MINUTES ✳ SERVES 2–3

Strip the coriander leaves from their stems, set aside the leaves as a garnish and put the stems in a medium saucepan. Bash the lemongrass stalks using the back of a rolling pin until broken and their strong aroma is released. Peel and cut the galangal into chunks and pound, again using a rolling pin, until a little liquid is released. Tear the lime leaves into smaller pieces. Smash the garlic. Put everything into the pan with the coriander stems, along with the chilli, shallots and palm sugar. Pour in the coconut milk. Place the pan over a medium heat and bring to a very gentle simmer. Cover with a lid and cook for 15 minutes.

Strain the soup through a sieve into another saucepan, discarding all the aromatics. Add the mushrooms, beans, lime juice, fish sauce and about 300ml of hot water until it is the right consistency – you want the soup to be light but still creamy. Bring the soup up to a light simmer again for 5–6 minutes, just to cook the mushrooms and edamame slightly. Season to taste and serve in bowls immediately, garnished with the coriander leaves, a slice of chilli, extra lime and lime leaves. Serve with steamed rice.

warm mung bean, cavolo, pancetta & walnut salad

INGREDIENTS
250g mung beans, soaked
   overnight and drained
200g smoked pancetta,
   thinly sliced
A glug of olive oil
200g bunch of cavolo nero,
   shredded
Small handful of flat-leaf
   parsley, finely chopped
Salt and freshly ground
   black pepper

FOR THE CANDIED WALNUTS
75g caster sugar
100g walnuts, toasted

FOR THE DRESSING
3 tablespoons olive oil
2 tablespoons cider vinegar
1 teaspoon Dijon mustard

The caramelised walnuts are important here as the sugar melts into the salad making for a sweet dressing. Once you've got the caramelising technique, it can be applied to all sorts of nuts and used both in sweet and savoury recipes. See page 94 for recipe photograph.

PREP TIME 10 MINUTES + OVERNIGHT SOAKING ✳ COOK TIME 35 MINUTES ✳ SERVES 4–6

Rinse the drained mung beans under cold running water and tip into a large saucepan. Cover with twice their volume of fresh water and simmer, uncovered, occasionally skimming the surface, until the beans are al dente – about 30 minutes but check after 25 minutes. Drain and season generously.

Meanwhile, fry the pancetta in a large dry frying pan over a high heat. Once crispy, remove and set aside. Add the oil to the hot pan, keep it on a medium-high heat and throw in the calvero nero. Cook for 2–3 minutes until the leaves are just starting to collapse. Stir in the cooked mung beans and most of the parsley, then turn off the heat. Cover to keep the beans warm.

To make the candied walnuts, put 75ml of cold water and the sugar into a small saucepan and boil together over a high heat for 6–7 minutes until the consistency becomes thick and syrupy. Add the walnuts to the pan. Keeping the heat high, cook the mixture, stirring constantly with a spatula or wooden spoon. As the sugar caramelises and the walnuts begin to toast, remove the pan from the heat and continue to stir vigorously until sugar crystals start to form around the nuts – they will start to take on a white, almost snowy, appearance. Spoon the dry candied nuts onto a chopping board or sheet of baking paper to cool slightly.

Make the dressing by combining the oil, vinegar, mustard. Season to taste and pour the dressing over the warm beans and cavolo nero, then toss gently. Turn out onto a platter and scatter over the pancetta, walnuts and any remaining parsley.

roasted carrot, lentil & feta salad

2 large carrots, scrubbed and
  cut into 4–5cm slices, on
  the diagonal
300g baby carrots, scrubbed
  clean and left whole
3 tablespoons olive oil
1 teaspoon coriander seeds
1 teaspoon cumin seeds
Small handful of thyme
200g feta cheese, broken
  into large, bite-sized chunks
400g can green lentils,
  drained
Juice of ½ lemon
4 tablespoons roughly
  chopped coriander leaves
Salt and freshly ground
  black pepper

Make this salad in summer when carrots are in season and at their best. This dish is substantial enough to eat as a main course, alongside a chunk of fresh bread, but would be lovely with a late summer barbecue.

PREP TIME 5 MINUTES ✳ COOK TIME 35–40 MINUTES ✳ SERVES 4

Preheat the oven to 180°C/160°C fan/gas mark 4.

Put the carrots, half the oil, the coriander and cumin seeds and thyme in a large baking tray. Season with salt and black pepper and roast for 15 minutes. Remove the tray and place the feta chunks on top of the carrots. Drizzle with a little more of the oil and season again with black pepper. Return the tray to the oven and roast for a further 20–25 minutes, or until the carrots are golden and the feta is soft and slightly wobbly.

Towards the end of the cooking time, warm the lentils in a small saucepan over a moderate heat. Stir through the remaining oil, lemon juice and coriander. Season to taste.

Spoon the lentils onto a serving platter and top with the roasted carrots and feta.

soft split pea, lemon & mint dip

175g dried green split peas
100g cream cheese
½ ripe avocado
Juice of ½ lemon
1 garlic clove, chopped
Handful of mint, roughly
  chopped
1 tablespoon olive oil
Salt and freshly ground
  black pepper

Breadsticks or crostini,
  to serve

I stumbled upon this recipe. Some over-zealous cooking of split peas rendered them perfect for blending – an ideal framework for this soft, summery, soft purée. You could dip in carrots or celery for an ideal pre-dinner warm-up.

PREP TIME 10 MINUTES ✳ COOK TIME 25–30 MINUTES ✳ SERVES 4

Bring a large saucepan of salted water to the boil over a medium heat. Add the split peas and cook at a brisk simmer for 25–30 minutes until the peas are just tender. Squash them between your fingers to see if they give a little. Drain and refresh under cold running water. Allow to cool completely.

Tip the split peas into the bowl of a food processor along with cream cheese, avocado, lemon juice, garlic, most of the mint, the oil and 1 tablespoon of cold water. Whizz until smooth, adding a touch more water if needed, to achieve a soft, spreadable consistency. Spoon into a bowl and top with the remaining mint. Serve in a bowl with breadsticks or crostini.

baked squash with coconut, coriander & lentils

INGREDIENTS

300g butternut squash, ideally the base end that holds the seeds

2 tablespoons olive oil, plus a little extra for brushing and drizzling

2 onions, finely sliced

3 large garlic cloves, sliced

1 large green chilli, sliced into rounds

1 teaspoon ground coriander

400g can green lentils, drained and rinsed

160ml coconut cream

Freshly chopped coriander, to garnish

Salt and freshly ground black pepper

This recipe was developed as all recipes should be, with friends in the kitchen and a pile of ingredients that needed shaping. The lentils are rich, thick with coconut milk and gently spiced – a suitable base for sweet roasted squash. Serve, as I did, warm from the oven with dressed, seasonal leaves.

PREP TIME 20 MINUTES ✳ **COOK TIME 1 HOUR** ✳ **SERVES 4**

Preheat the oven to 200°C/180°C fan/gas mark 6. Line a baking sheet with greaseproof paper.

Prepare the squash by peeling the skin using a vegetable peeler and slicing into 2cm rounds, removing any seeds – aim for five slices. Brush each round with oil and lay on the prepared baking sheet. Roast for 25 minutes, turning halfway through, until soft.

Meanwhile, heat the oil in a large, heavy-based frying pan. Add the onions and gently fry over a medium heat for 4–5 minutes until soft and golden. Add the garlic, chilli and ground coriander and fry for a further 3–4 minutes. Add the lentils and combine. Stir through the coconut cream with 3 tablespoons of cold water and season generously.

Transfer the mixture to a 2-litre ovenproof dish. Remove the squash from the oven and nestle the rounds into the lentil mixture. Return to the oven and bake for a further 25 minutes. Remove from the oven and scatter over a little fresh coriander. Serve with a little extra drizzle of oil, if liked.

green lentil, pak choy & spring onion salad

INGREDIENTS

150g dried green lentils
1 tablespoon sesame oil
2 pak choy, cut into quarters
3 spring onions, roughly
   chopped
Small bunch of garlic chives
   or chives, chopped

FOR THE DRESSING

Juice of 1 lime
1½ tablespoons rice wine
   vinegar
2 tablespoons sesame oil
1 teaspoon light soy sauce
1 teaspoon runny honey
3cm piece of ginger, peeled
   and finely grated
1 red chilli, finely chopped
Salt and freshly ground
   black pepper

The leafy bulbs of pak choy find themselves in our fridge more and more often, such is their popularity at home (and particularly when fried and fused with nutty sesame oil). Simply wilt, combine with soft lentils, softened spring onions and a tart soy dressing and pull this salad together in minutes.

PREP TIME 15 MINUTES ✳ **COOK TIME 30 MINUTES**
✳ **SERVES 4 AS A LIGHT LUNCH OR SIDE**

Bring a large saucepan of salted water to the boil and tip in the lentils. Reduce the heat to a simmer and cook for 25 minutes, stirring from time to time, until the lentils are just soft. Drain and keep warm.

Meanwhile, make the dressing. Combine the lime juice, rice wine vinegar, sesame oil, soy sauce and honey in a jar with a tight-fitting lid. Shake until well combined before adding the ginger – and any juices – and chilli. Taste and season.

Heat the sesame oil in a large frying pan or wok over a high heat. Gently stir-fry the pak choy for 3–5 minutes until slightly collapsed. Remove from the pan and add the spring onions to the pan, frying for 3–4 minutes until wilted. Combine the warm lentils, pak choy, spring onions and dressing in a shallow bowl and spoon onto a serving plate. Garnish with a flurry of chives.

green lentil risotto

INGREDIENTS

40g unsalted butter

2 tablespoons olive oil

1 red onion, finely sliced

1 onion, finely sliced

Small bunch of spring
onions, finely sliced

3 garlic cloves, crushed

300g dried green lentils,
rinsed

900ml hot chicken or
vegetable stock

200ml white wine

150g Wensleydale cheese or
feta, crumbled

Small bunch of chives,
chopped

Salt and freshly ground
black pepper

Not strictly speaking a risotto as you will notice the lack of arborio rice, but the method of slowly adding stock to the lentils is the same. Do take your time to soften the onions – the texture becomes soft and delectable, keep going until the lentils collapse a little. Trust me, the combination of cheese, onions and soft lentils is deeply satisfying.

PREP TIME 20 MINUTES ✳ COOK TIME 50–60 MINUTES ✳ SERVES 4

Heat half the butter and the oil in a large, heavy-based saucepan or casserole. Add all three types of onion and gently sauté over a low heat for 15 minutes, or until softened, golden and slightly sticky. Stir through the garlic and cook for a further 2 minutes. Add the wine and continue to cook until the liquid has all but evaporated. Stir the green lentils into the mixture and gently combine.

Pour the stock over the lentils and increase the heat to a simmer. Stir the mixture fairly regularly for 35–40 minutes, or until the liquid has reduced by two-thirds and the lentils have begun to break down. The consistency should be soft and slightly creamy. Stir through the cheese and chives and remove the 'risotto' from the heat. Adjust the seasoning as necessary and serve with nothing but fresh salad leaves.

white fish with warm lentil & beetroot salad

INGREDIENTS

250g dried green lentils,
  rinsed
4 tablespoons olive oil
1 tablespoon white wine
  vinegar
Bunch of beetroot, peeled
  and cut into wedges
2 Cox's apples, cored and
  sliced into 8 wedges
2 banana shallots, quartered
2 garlic cloves, lightly
  bashed
Handful of flat-leaf parsley,
  finely chopped
4 x 170g sustainably sourced
  white fish fillets (such as
  coley, whiting or pollack),
  boned
1 tablespoon capers,
  chopped
Salt and freshly ground
  black pepper

FOR THE HORSERADISH CREAM

1½ tablespoons fresh
  horseradish, finely
  grated (or use creamed
  horseradish)
120ml crème fraîche

One of the simplest and perhaps most effective method of cooking fillets is to pan-fry them. If done correctly, the flesh should be soft and tender and the skin crisp. The warm lentil and beetroot salad flatters the fish without being too overbearing.

PREP TIME 30 MINUTES ✳ **COOK TIME 1 HOUR** ✳ **SERVES 4**

Preheat the oven to 200°C/180°C fan/gas mark 6.

Tip the lentils into a large, deep saucepan and cover with twice their volume of cold water. Salt and bring to a rolling boil, then reduce the heat to a gentle simmer and cook for 15–20 minutes, until the lentils are al dente. Remove from the heat and drain. Return the lentils to the pan and, while still warm, stir through 2 tablespoons of the oil and the vinegar. Season to taste and keep warm.

Meanwhile, put the prepared beetroot, shallots, garlic, half the parsley and 1 tablespoon of oil in a medium roasting dish. Cover the dish with foil and roast for 40 minutes, tossing around halfway through cooking. The veg are cooked when you can insert a metal skewer into the beetroot with little pressure and the shallots have softened. Discard the foil, add the apple wedges into the dish and roast for a further 10 minutes until the apples have lost their structure. Remove and set aside.

Combine the warm lentils with the beetroot mixture and capers, then set aside.

Heat a little oil in a non-stick frying pan until almost smoking hot. Season the fish fillets and add them to the hot oil, skin-side down, and cook for 4 minutes. Gently turn over and cook for 4 minutes more until golden and just cooked through.

Meanwhile, make the horseradish cream. Combine the horseradish and crème fraîche and season to taste. Divide the lentils and fish between four plates and top with the horseradish cream and the remaining dill.

Serve the warm lentil salad alongside the pan fried fish and horseradish cream.

ribollita with green lentils & tuscan sausage

INGREDIENTS

A generous glug of olive oil, plus extra to drizzle

2 onions, finely chopped

4 garlic cloves, crushed

2 carrots, finely chopped

2 celery sticks, finely chopped

½ teaspoon crushed dried chillies

Small bunch of oregano, chopped

4 anchovy fillets, finely chopped

400g can Puy lentils, drained

400g can chopped tomatoes

100ml hot vegetable stock

Zest of 1 unwaxed lemon

2 bay leaves

150g stale bread, torn into chunks

4 Tuscan sausages

Salt and freshly ground black pepper

Ribollita, the infamous vibrant, flavourful Tuscan soup that is bulked out with yesterday's bread. My version includes a meaty Italian sausage, which moves it from the soup-but-may-need-more bracket to a full, rounded supper.

PREP TIME 25 MINUTES ✳ COOK TIME 40 MINUTES ✳ SERVES 4–6

Heat the oil in a large deep-sided saucepan over a low heat and add the onions, garlic, carrots and celery. Fry the vegetables for a good 20 minutes, adding the chillies, oregano and anchovies halfway through, until all are soft and steamy. Stir through the lentils, tomatoes and stock and increase the heat to a simmer. Stir through the lemon zest, bay leaves and stale bread and cook over a low–medium heat, uncovered, for a further 20 minutes, adding a touch of cold water if needed, to achieve your desired consistancy. The soup should be thick and stew-like.

Meanwhile, cook the sausages. Heat a little oil in a small frying pan and gently fry the sausages over a medium heat, turning regularly, for 12–14 minutes until golden brown and cooked through. Drain on kitchen paper.

Season the soup to taste. Slice each sausage in half at an angle and ladle the soup into bowls. Top each with two halves of a sausage and a drizzle of oil.

pan-fried cod, green split peas & new potato fries

INGREDIENTS

700g new potatoes, washed
350g green split peas,
    soaked overnight in cold
    water with ½ tablespoon
    lemon juice
Unsalted butter, for frying
2–3 tablespoons olive oil
3 shallots, finely chopped
Juice of 1 lemon
Large handful of finely
    chopped mint
4 cod fillets, preferably
    sustainable, skin on
Salt and freshly ground
    black pepper

FOR THE TARTARE

150ml crème fraîche
1 tablespoon chopped soft
    herbs (such as mint,
    parsley and dill fronds)
1 teaspoon capers, chopped
3 small gherkins, finely
    chopped

Cod and mushy peas – a combination that we all need once a season, at least. The peas are delicious, cooked with mint, shallots and olive oil and blended until perfectly soft.

PREP TIME 30 MINUTES ✳ **COOK TIME 50 MINUTES** ✳ **SERVES 4**

Put the potatoes in a medium saucepan of cold salted water over a high heat and bring to the boil. Boil for 10–12 minutes until a knife is easily inserted. Drain and thickly slice. Set aside.

Next, tip the green split peas into a medium saucepan and cover with cold water. Bring to a rolling boil, reduce the heat to a simmer and cook the peas for 25–30 minutes until they are soft but still al dente. Drain and set aside.

Melt the butter in a large frying pan. When it is foaming, add half the sliced potatoes and season well. Cook over a medium heat for about 15 minutes until the potatoes turn golden brown and crispy. Remove from the pan and set aside to keep warm. Repeat this process with the remaining potatoes.

Make the tartare sauce by mixing all the ingredients together, then season.

Heat the oil in another large frying pan over a medium heat. Add the shallots and sweat for a few minutes until soft and slightly golden. Toss the warm peas into the pan with the lemon juice, mint and a little more oil. Season to taste. Set aside and keep warm.

Finally, cook the cod. Pat the fillets dry with kitchen paper, removing any excess moisture. Heat a large, non-stick frying pan over a medium heat and add a good knob of butter. Put the fillets in the pan, skin-side down, and fry the fish, without nudging or moving it, for a minute or so. Lift gently, to check the skin – it should be slightly crisping. Turn the fish over and season. Reduce the heat slightly and cook for a further 3–4 minutes until the flesh is opaque and cooked through.

Serve the cod on a bed of the soft peas, with the crispy potatoes and dollop of the crème fraîche tartare.

baked chicken, green split peas, leek & chorizo bake

INGREDIENTS

250g green split peas, rinsed
2 tablespoon olive oil
450g skinless, boneless
  chicken thighs, quartered
2 leeks, trimmed and cut
  into 1.5cm rounds
2 garlic cloves, sliced
250ml full-fat crème fraîche
2 tablespoons chopped mint
100g feta cheese, crumbled
100g chorizo, sliced
Salt and freshly ground
  black pepper

I cooked this for my beautiful friend Annabel. We had been working together all day and needed a simple supper, with little admin required, to enjoy once the computers had been switched off. This was it: unpretentious chicken thighs made brilliant with the addition of split peas, chorizo, plenty of mint and golden baked feta.

PREP TIME 25 MINUTES ✳ **COOK TIME 1 HOUR 30 MINUTES** ✳ **SERVES 6–8**

Bring a large saucepan of water to the boil, tip in the split peas and simmer for 45 minutes – they should still have a nutty bite to them. Keep topping up with fresh water if the water evaporates too much.

Meanwhile, heat half the oil in a large frying pan over a high heat. Add the chicken thighs and fry until the edges begin to turn golden; the chicken doesn't have to be completely cooked through at this stage. Remove the chicken from the pan, add a touch more oil to the pan if needed and add the leeks. Reduce the heat to medium and fry for 5–6 minutes until softened. Add in the garlic for the final minute, just taking the edge off it.

Preheat the oven to 180°C/160°C fan/gas mark 4.

Tip the chicken, leeks and peas into a generous mixing bowl and combine. Season well and stir through the crème fraîche and mint. Transfer everything into a greased 2-litre ovenproof serving dish.

Top with the feta and chorizo. Bake for 30 minutes until all is bubbling and the chicken is completely cooked through. Remove and leave to stand for 5 minutes. Serve with salad leaves.

yellow

SOYA BEANS

✳

YELLOW SPLIT PEAS

✳

CHICKPEAS

homemade soya milk with oats & strawberries

INGREDIENTS
100g dried soya beans

FOR THE PORRIDGE
200ml soya milk
100g rolled oats, plus 30g
  extra for the topping
1 tablespoon coconut oil
50g strawberries or
  raspberries

You will also need a square
  of muslin

There are many good reasons to avoid dairy (being vegan or lactose intolerant are top of the list) and soya milk is a nutritious, cost-effective and adaptable replacement. Making it is a slight labour of love, but once done, it can be used in a number of ways. Here, it's poured onto oats and allowed to soak for an hour or so before being eaten with fresh berries. Serve with coffee.

PREP TIME 25 MINUTES + 19 HOURS SOAKING ✳ **COOK TIME 30 MINUTES** ✳ **SERVES 2**

Put the soya beans into a large bowl, cover with twice their volume of cold water and leave to soak for 18 hours. Keep your eye on the water level, topping up slightly if needed – these beans seem to drink water. The beans have soaked enough if they give a little when squeezed between finger and thumb.

Rinse thoroughly and drain the beans and transfer them to a blender with 750ml of cold water. Purée until very smooth. Line a large bowl with muslin and pour the mixture into the bowl. Gather up all four corners of the muslin and twist and squeeze out as much liquid as possible, discarding the pulp.

Pour the soya milk into a large saucepan with a further 500ml of cold water and bring to a simmer over a moderately low heat, stirring constantly to avoid scorching. Continue to heat for 20–25 minutes. Allow the soya milk to cool and keep in the fridge for 3–4 days.

Once ready to assemble the porridge, simply pour 200ml of the fresh soya milk over the oats and leave to stand for 1 hour, until the liquid has all but disappeared.

Meanwhile, heat the coconut oil in a small frying pan over a medium-high heat. Once melted, stir through the extra 30g of oats and toast for 2–3 minutes until just crunchy. Serve the soaked oats in small bowls, studded with the strawberries and topped with the coconut oats.

poached chicken, soya bean & herby pancetta salad

INGREDIENTS

1.3kg whole free-range
    chicken,
1.5 litres milk
5 black peppercorns
2 thyme sprigs
150g soya beans, soaked
    for 16 hours, drained
    and rinsed
Zest of 1 unwaxed lemon
1 tablespoon olive oil
Salt and freshly ground
    black pepper

FOR THE DRESSING

120ml buttermilk
3 tablespoons mayonnaise
30ml whole milk
1 tablespoon lemon juice
½ bunch of parsley, finely
    chopped
½ bunch of chives, finely
    chopped
8 thin slices of pancetta
100g lamb's lettuce or pea
    shoots
5–6 radishes, thinly sliced

Soya beans, mostly known for their ability to mimic meat in tofu or TVP (Textured Vegetable Protein), can very well stand on their own when needed. Here, served with a buttermilk dressing, salad leaves and softly poached chicken, they make for a lovely summer partnership.

PREP TIME 45 MINUTES ✷ COOK TIME 1 HOUR ✷ SERVES 6 AS A LIGHT LUNCH

To poach the chicken, place the whole bird in a large, tall saucepan or stockpot. Add the milk, peppercorns and thyme and bring the pot to a simmer. Skim off any froth that floats to the surface, then leave at a low simmer for 1 hour 15 minutes, until the chicken is plump, soft and cooked all the way through. Remove from the pot, transfer to a board and set aside to cool for a few minutes. Once cooled, gently pull the chicken meat away from the bones in generous-sized pieces. Set aside.

Meanwhile, bring a large saucepan of salted water to the boil and add the soya beans. Reduce the heat to a simmer for 45 minutes or until the beans are just tender. Strain and add to a medium bowl along with the lemon zest and olive oil, toss together and season to taste.

Make the dressing by gently whisking together the buttermilk, mayonnaise, milk and lemon juice. Stir through the herbs and season to taste. Set aside.

Heat a large heavy-based frying pan or griddle pan over a high heat until really hot. Add the pancetta to the pan and cook on either side for 3 minutes or until golden brown and curling at the edges. I love the pancetta when it's really crispy. Pat dry using kitchen paper.

To assemble the salad, toss together the poached chicken and soya beans. Layer up handfuls of lamb's lettuce and radishes on a serving plate. Drizzle over half the dressing. Top with the chicken and the remaining dressing. Finally, crumble over shards of crispy pancetta.

spiced cauliflower & split pea curry with clove rice

INGREDIENTS

200g yellow split peas

3 tablespoons sunflower oil

1 large cauliflower head, base trimmed and florets broken off

3 banana shallots, thinly sliced

Thumb-sized piece of ginger, peeled and grated

3 large garlic cloves, crushed

½ green chilli, finely chopped

3 teaspoons ground cumin

1 teaspoon turmeric powder

1 teaspoon nigella seeds (black onion seeds)

400ml coconut milk

400g can chopped tomatoes

1 cinnamon stick

Juice of 1 lime

Salt and freshly ground black pepper

FOR THE RICE

300g basmati rice, rinsed

1 teaspoon whole cloves

1 bay leaf

FOR THE TOPPING

1 teaspoon sunflower oil

1 tablespoon cumin seeds

30g flaked almonds, toasted

A delicate curry, but with a nip of pungency and brightness. A simple clove rice completes the meal.

PREP TIME 30 MINUTES ✳ COOK TIME 1 HOUR 10 MINUTES ✳ SERVES 4

Bring a large saucepan of salted water to the boil and add the split peas, reduce the heat to a simmer and cook for 45–55 minutes, until soft with a little bite. Strain and set aside.

Heat a glug of oil in a large, heavy-based casserole over a medium heat. Add the cauliflower florets to the pan and fry for 5–7 minutes, or until beginning to turn golden brown around the edges. Remove from the pan and set aside.

Add the remaining oil to the pan and gently fry the shallots over a medium heat for 5 minutes until soft and slightly golden. Stir through the ginger, garlic and chilli and fry for a further 1–2 minutes before adding the cumin, turmeric and nigella seeds. Cook for a final minute. Pour over the coconut milk and tomatoes with the cinnamon stick. Return the cauliflower to the pan along with the peas. As soon as the curry comes to the boil, cover with a lid and reduce the heat to a simmer so the cauliflower cooks gently for about 20 minutes. The cauliflower should be tender and the peas soft and creamy. Fish out the cinnamon stick, squeeze in the lime juice and season to taste.

Meanwhile, cook the rice. Put the rice in a large saucepan along with the cloves and bay leaf. Cover with roughly twice the volume of cold water. Bring to the boil, then reduce the heat to a simmer and cover the pan with a lid. Cook gently for about 15 minutes, or until all the water has been absorbed. If the water has absorbed but the rice still doesn't seem to be cooked, top it up with a little more boiling water. Once cooked, cover with a lid and allow to sit for 5 minutes. Remove the aromatics and fluff up with a fork.

To make the topping, heat the oil in a small saucepan. Add the cumin seeds and almonds and fry for 3 minutes or until the seeds begin to pop.

Serve the cauliflower curry alongside the clove rice. Top with the cumin seeds, toasted almonds and extra lime wedges for squeezing, if you wish.

yellow dhal with jewelled red onion & mint topping

INGREDIENTS

400g yellow split peas,
  rinsed
2 curry leaves
3 large garlic cloves, bashed
1 small red chilli, halved
Thumb-sized piece of
  ginger, peeled
70ml chopped tomatoes
4 tablespoons olive oil
3 large banana shallots,
  finely sliced
1 teaspoon mustard seeds
1 teaspoon ground cumin
1 teaspoon turmeric powder
½ teaspoon garam masala
1 teaspoon brown sugar
A generous handful of
  coriander leaves, roughly
  chopped
A generous handful of mint
  leaves, roughly chopped
1 red onion, finely chopped

Dhal is the sort of recipe that fits an 'everyday' bracket. This protein-rich, spice-rich and flavourful dhal particularly enjoys the fresh bite of the topping, necessary as much for the added texture as the flavour.

PREP TIME 30 MINUTES ✳ **COOK TIME 2 HOURS 30 MINUTES** ✳ **SERVES 6–8**

Put the rinsed split peas in a large saucepan. Cover with 2 litres of cold water and bring to the boil, reduce the heat to a simmer and add the curry leaves, garlic, chilli and ginger. Cook gently for 1½–2 hours, or until the dhal has broken down and is smooth and creamy. Add a little more boiling water if necessary to loosen – you're looking for a thick soup-like consistency. Discard the curry leaves, garlic, chilli and ginger. Stir through the tomatoes and cook for a further 10 minutes, season to taste and set aside for a little while.

Heat 2 tablespoons of the olive oil in a large casserole dish or saucepan over a low heat. Add the shallots and cook gently for 8–10 minutes, or until beginning to soften. Add the mustard seeds, cumin, turmeric and garam masala and cook for a further 3 minutes. Stir the spiced shallots through your dhal. Continue to simmer for 10 minutes. Stir through the brown sugar and half the coriander.

Serve the dhal topped with the remaining coriander, the mint and red onion and drizzle with the remaining olive oil.

mixed dhal chaat

INGREDIENTS

200g yellow split peas,
  soaked in water for 2 hours
  then drained
300ml sunflower or
  vegetable oil, for frying
1 teaspoon ground cumin
1½ teaspoons chaat masala
2 small red onions, finely
  diced
3 medium tomatoes,
  deseeded and finely diced
½ cucumber, deseeded and
  finely diced
Juice of ½ lemon
Large handful of coriander,
  chopped
2 tablespoons thick natural
  yogurt
salt and freshly ground
  black pepper

Chaat masala, a blend of spices and amchoor – dried mango powder – binds this bright, multi-layered street-food salad of split peas or lentils, crispy fried onion and watery, cool cucumber. You can also use red split lentils or chana dal (split chickpeas) for this recipe, but check cooking times. Serve a small portion to accompany a meaty curry or choose to champion the dhal in deep bowls with a doughy naan.

PREP TIME 20 MINUTES + 2 HOURS SOAKING ✳ COOK TIME 45 MINUTES ✳ SERVES 2–3

Bring a large saucepan of water to a rolling boil. Salt and add the lentils to the pan. Cook for 25–30 minutes, or until the lentils are soft but still retain a little bite (they will have a second cooking). Drain well and pat dry with kitchen paper.

Heat the oil in a medium saucepan over a medium heat until it just reaches smoking point. Working in batches, add the lentils and deep-fry for 3–5 minutes. Remove and dry on kitchen paper while you cook the remainder. Toss the lentils in the cumin and masala powder, season to taste and set aside.

Toss together the onions, tomatoes, cucumber, lemon juice and coriander. Layer the vegetables and deep-fried lentils into two or three bowls. Combine each using a swift stir of a spoon so the layers are barely muddled. Top with the yogurt.

soft herb hummus

400g can chickpeas, drained
  and rinsed
3 tablespoons tahini
1 large garlic clove, crushed
Zest and juice of 1 lemon
2 tablespoons olive oil
½ bunch of basil, finely
  chopped
½ bunch of dill, finely
  chopped
½ bunch of flat-leaf parsley,
  finely chopped
Salt and freshly ground
  black pepper

Hummus can vary dramatically, and I fear we've all become accustomed to a mass-produced, mayonnaise-heavy, slurry version and left behind the authentic Middle Eastern form. And yet making your own is so easy – once you've bought a jar of tahini you're more than halfway there. Sling together chickpeas, lemon juice, garlic, tahini and a healthy glug of olive oil and create chickpea perfection. This version contains plenty of soft herbs, which add another dimension to this classic dip.

PREP TIME 10 MINUTES ✳ SERVES 4–6

Tip the chickpeas, tahini, garlic and lemon zest and juice into a food processor and blend to a coarse purée. Drizzle the olive oil and 3–4 tablespoons water into the mixture and continue to blend until you have a good, spreadable consistency. Check the seasoning and stir through the herbs.

beetroot, buttermilk & dill hummus

400g can chickpeas, drained
  and rinsed
200g cooked beetroot,
  chopped
3 tablespoons tahini
1 large garlic clove, crushed
70–80ml buttermilk
1 tablespoon poppy seeds
2 tablespoons finely
  chopped dill fronds
Salt and freshly ground
  black pepper

PREP TIME 15 MINUTES ✳ SERVES 4–6

Put the chickpeas, beetroot, tahini, garlic and half the buttermilk into a food processor and blitz until smooth. Season to taste. Serve, garnished with the remaining buttermilk swirled on top. Finish with the poppy seeds and dill.

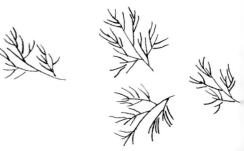

SOFT HERB HUMMUS

GREEN AVOCADO HUMMUS

BEETROOT, BUTTERMILK & DILL HUMMUS

CARAMELISED ONION & BLUE CHEESE HUMMUS

caramelised onion & blue cheese hummus

1 tablespoon olive oil
2 red onions, finely sliced
1 tablespoon soft brown
  sugar
1 tablespoon balsamic
  vinegar
1 tablespoon red wine
  vinegar
400g can chickpeas, drained
  and rinsed
3 tablespoons tahini
1 large garlic clove, crushed
Zest and juice of 1 lemon
50g blue cheese, finely
  crumbled
2 tablespoons coriander
  seeds, toasted
Salt and black pepper

PREP TIME 10 MINUTES ✳ COOK TIME 15 MINUTES ✳ SERVES 4–6

Heat the oil in a medium frying pan over a medium heat, then add the onions and cook gently for 6–8 minutes, or until soft and slightly golden. Add the sugar and both vinegars and cook for a further 5 minutes until the liquid has almost been absorbed and the mixture has become sticky. Set aside.

Blitz the chickpeas, tahini, garlic and lemon zest and juice together in a food processor, until smooth. Transfer into a bowl and stir through the crumbled cheese and 4–5 tablespoons water to create a soft dropping consistency. Season to taste. Top the hummus with the caramelised onions and toasted coriander seeds.

green avocado hummus

400g can chickpeas, drained
  and rinsed
3 tablespoons tahini
1 large garlic clove, crushed
Zest and juice of 1 lemon
1 large ripe avocado, halved
  and stoned
1 tablespoon avocado oil or
  olive oil, to serve
Salt and freshly ground
  black pepper

PREP TIME 15 MINUTES ✳ COOK TIME 5 MINUTES ✳ SERVES 4–6

Blend the chickpeas, tahini, garlic and lemon zest and juice until smooth. Add the avocado flesh and blitz again until smooth, adding 2–3 tablespoons water if required for the right consistency. Taste and season; it will surely need a little salt. Serve with a drizzle of oil.

greek hummus
with yellow split peas

200g yellow split peas,
  rinsed
1 small onion, finely
  chopped
2 bay leaves
1–2 teaspoons sea salt
2 teaspoons red wine
  vinegar
Juice of 1 lemon
2–3 tablespoons olive oil

If you are a lover of hummus and let's face it, who isn't?, then this is a chance to switch up your routine. Despite the traditional name being 'Greek Fava', the dip is made with yellow split peas (actually fava beans are used very rarely in Greece because a significant chunk of the population is allergic to them). Use as a dip or, as the Greeks do, as a side to meat, fish or vegetable dishes.

PREP TIME 10 MINUTES ✳ COOK TIME 45 MINUTES ✳ SERVES 4–6

Put the rinsed split peas into a large saucepan with the onion, bay leaves and enough water to cover the split peas. Bring to the boil, then reduce the heat and simmer for 30–45 minutes until the split peas are thick and mushy – precise timings will depend on the age of the peas, so check after 30 minutes. If some water remains, drain it off before transferring the peas to a bowl. Discard the bay leaves.

Add the salt, vinegar and lemon juice to the softened peas and blitz with a hand-held blender until smooth, adding the olive oil for a spreading consistency. Taste to perfect the seasoning and serve in a large bowl.

coriander & cashew green falafel with harissa yogurt

INGREDIENTS

120g dried chickpeas,
 soaked overnight in plenty
 of water
120g dried fava beans,
 soaked overnight in plenty
 of water
2 tablespoons tahini
1 large garlic clove, crushed
1 teaspoon ground cumin
2 tablespoons chopped fresh
 coriander
3 teaspoons coriander seeds,
 lightly bashed
50g cashew nuts (or
 macadamia nuts), toasted
 and chopped
½ small green chilli, finely
 chopped
2–3 tablespoons sesame
 seeds
120ml sunflower oil, for
 frying
Salt and freshly ground
 black pepper

FOR THE HARISSA YOGURT

100g thick natural yogurt
1 shallot, very finely chopped
½ tablespoon harissa paste

Dried beans provide the right combo of starch and water for the mix to hold together, so do take the time to use these. You can't get fresh chickpeas and using tinned beans will make the mixture mushy, unless you add heaps of flour so that's that settled!

PREP TIME 15 MINUTES + SOAKING AND CHILLING ✳ COOK TIME 10 MINUTES ✳ MAKES 10–12 FALAFEL

Drain the chickpeas and fava beans, then rinse well under cold running water and leave to drip dry in a colander or sieve.

Put the drained pulses into a food processor and whizz until smooth. Add the tahini, garlic and cumin and pulse again, until well combined but still with some texture. Scoop the mixture into a bowl and stir through the fresh coriander, coriander seeds, cashew nuts and green chilli. Season with salt and pepper. Chill the mixture for at least 30 minutes, but leave for an hour, or two, if you have the time.

Get ahead by making the harissa yogurt. Mix the yogurt with the finely diced shallot and harissa paste. Season well.

Next, divide the falafel mixture into 16 smallish patties, flattening gently on either side using your palms. Roll lightly in the sesame seeds and set aside on a baking tray lined with baking paper.

Heat the sunflower oil in a heavy-based frying pan. Working in batches, fry the falafel for 3–4 minutes on either side until brown and crispy. Drain on kitchen paper to remove any excess oil and serve hot, alongside a bowlful of the harissa yogurt.

chickpea & spinach stew

INGREDIENTS

225g dried chickpeas
Pinch of bicarbonate of soda
100ml olive oil
4 garlic cloves, sliced
2 teaspoons Spanish sweet
  paprika
1 teaspoon ground cumin
Pinch of saffron strands
100g stale bread, cubed
2 tablespoons sherry vinegar
75g whole blanched almonds
500ml hot vegetable stock
150g spinach, washed and
  roughly chopped
Salt and freshly ground
  black pepper

Likely to be found on a tapas menu in Northern Spain, potaje garbanzos espinacas is a very traditional garlic soup, thickened with an unusual garlic fried breadcrumb and almond paste. Introduce sherry vinegar into your storecupboard if you aren't familiar with it – the slight sweetness is ideal for this soup, balancing nicely with the nutty paste and soft chickpeas.

PREP TIME 30 MINUTES + OVERNIGHT SOAKING ✳ COOK TIME 2 HOURS ✳ SERVES 6

The night before you want to make this stew, tip the chickpeas into a large bowl, add the bicarbonate of soda (apparently this helps reduce their gassy tendencies) and soak in twice their volume of cold water.

The following day, drain the chickpeas and tip them into a large saucepan. Cover with cold, unsalted water and bring to the boil. Reduce the heat slightly and boil, uncovered, for 2 hours until the beans are tender. Drain well and return to the pan.

Meanwhile, heat the oil in a large heavy-based frying pan over a moderate heat. Once shimmering, fry the sliced garlic until soft. Fish out the garlic from the pan using a slotted spoon, add the spices to the oil and cook for 1 minute. Throw the bread into the oil. Fry the cubes for 2 minutes, or until golden and crispy and, using the slotted spoon, remove and set aside with the garlic until the chickpeas are cooked.

Blend the fried bread, garlic, vinegar and blanched almonds to a thick crumb. Add the stock to the cooked chickpeas and stir through the spinach. Cover the pan with a lid and allow the leaves to wilt before stirring through the bread paste. Season to taste and serve in warmed bowls.

goan coconut fish curry

FOR THE CURRY PASTE

30g cashew nuts

3 shallots, chopped

1 large red chilli, chopped

2 garlic cloves, chopped

2 tablespoons grated fresh
ginger

1 tablespoon white wine
vinegar

Medium bunch of coriander

FOR THE CURRY

2 tablespoons sunflower oil

1 red pepper, sliced

1 teaspoon turmeric powder

½ teaspoon ground
coriander

½ teaspoon hot chilli powder

5 curry leaves

400ml can coconut milk

160ml coconut cream

400g can chickpeas, drained
and rinsed

100g baby spinach

200g raw peeled prawns

200g cod fillet, skinned and
cut into chunks

2 teaspoons mustard seeds

Juice of 1 lime

Fresh fish and rich-tasting coconut take up spices beautifully in this fragrant broth. This recipe has a traditional Goan edge with the additional sour ingredient, sometimes tamarind but in this case vinegar. Eat from a deep bowl fresh with the final flurry of coriander leaves and a squeeze of lime juice.

PREP TIME 20 MINUTES ✳ COOK TIME 30 MINUTES ✳ SERVES 4

To make the curry paste, toast the cashew nuts in a dry frying pan until just charred, then remove from the heat and put into a blender or food processor with the shallots, chilli, garlic, ginger, vinegar and half the coriander. Blitz to a thick mush, adding a little water until you have a loose, aromatic paste. Scrape into a small bowl.

To make the curry, heat the oil in a large heavy-based frying pan over a medium heat and add the red peppers while the oil warms. Cook for about 5 minutes until beginning to soften. Once the peppers have collapsed, stir through the curry paste and continue to fry gently for a further few minutes. Add the spices and stir again – keep the heat up while they cook for another minute or so.

Add the curry leaves, coconut milk and cream and 100ml cold water. Increase the heat and bring to the boil, before lowering the temperature and simmering for 10–15 minutes. Add the chickpeas and cook gently for a further 5 minutes.

Finally add the spinach, prawns and cod to the pan and poach for 2–3 minutes until the fish is just opaque. Garnish with the mustard seeds and the remaining coriander and squeeze over some lime juice to serve.

white chocolate, coconut & vanilla-bean roasted chickpeas

400g can chickpeas, drained
  and rinsed
3 tablespoons coconut oil
½ teaspoon fine sea salt
300g white chocolate,
  broken into pieces
1 teaspoon vanilla bean
  paste
50g dried cranberries
40g shelled pistachios,
  sliced

Chickpeas are roasted in coconut oil until nutty brown and strewn over melted chocolate with cranberries and green pistachio nuts. This is chocolate in its element. Break into jagged pieces and hand out as an after-dinner treat.

PREP TIME 10 MINUTES ✳ **COOK TIME 40 MINUTES** ✳ **MAKES ENOUGH FOR 10**

Preheat the oven to 180°C/ 160°C/ gas mark 4. Pat the rinsed chickpeas with kitchen paper. Tip them into a large roasting tray and toss with the coconut oil and sea salt. Roast on the middle shelf of the oven for 30–40 minutes or until the chickpeas turn golden brown and slightly crunchy. Line a baking tray with a sheet of baking parchment. Put the white chocolate and vanilla paste into a bowl over a saucepan of simmering water and allow to melt gently – this should take 5–10 minutes. Remove from the heat and stir half the chickpeas into the melted chocolate mixture. Pour the chocolate onto the parchment and, using a palette knife, spread it slightly. Scatter with the remaining chickpeas, cranberries and pistachios and place the tray somewhere cool to allow the 'bark' to set. Once hard, break into shards and serve with coffee after dinner.

salted caramel & cinnamon roasted chickpeas

2 x 400g cans good-quality
  large chickpeas, drained
  and rinsed
2 tablespoons olive oil
60g unsalted butter
70g soft brown sugar
2 teaspoons fine sea salt
1 teaspoon ground cinnamon

It turns out the familiar chickpea can be transformed from a savoury staple to a sweet, crispy and delectable treat. Eat as they are or make a batch and use to dress up yogurt, fool or a soft ice cream.

PREP TIME 10 MINUTES ✳ **COOK TIME 30 MINUTES** ✳ **MAKES A GOOD BOWLFUL**

Preheat the oven to 180°C/ 160°C/ gas mark 4. Pat dry the chickpeas with kitchen paper. Tip them into a large roasting tray and toss with the oil. Roast on the middle shelf of the oven for 30–40 minutes, or until the chickpeas look golden and roasted and have a little crunch to them.

Meanwhile, melt the butter in a small saucepan over a medium heat. Combine the warm butter with the sugar, sea salt and cinnamon. Remove the chickpeas from the oven and transfer to a large bowl. Pour over the cinnamon butter mixture and gently combine until everything is well coated. Allow to cool. Serve as a snack or atop natural yogurt.

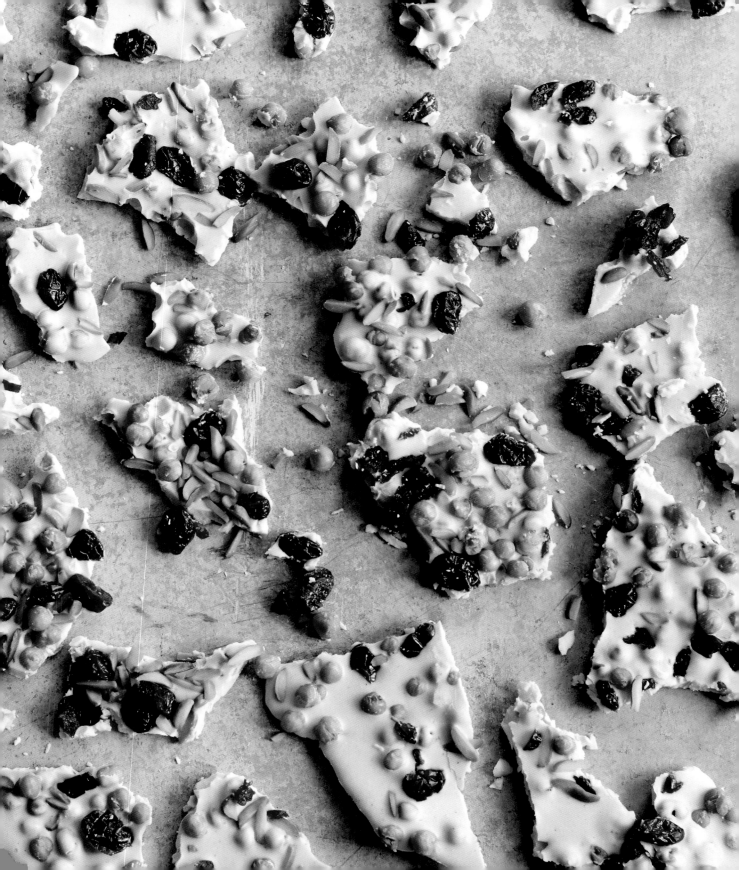

apple & chickpea cake

INGREDIENTS

sunflower oil, for greasing

400g can chickpeas, drained and rinsed

3 medium eggs

2 teaspoons almond essence

225g self-raising flour

1 tablespoon baking powder

175g caster sugar

500g (about 3) cooking apples, peeled, cored and cut into 2–4cm chunks

25g flaked almonds

25g demerara sugar

3 tablespoons apricot jam, warmed (optional)

The ratio of apples to cake in this recipe is high, resulting in a familiar soft, fudgy texture, almost akin to a pudding cake. The almond essence is a necessity – it sends a pleasing marzipan tone through the sponge and apricot glaze. The apricot glaze is an optional step but makes the home cook feel quite the professional.

PREP TIME 25 MINUTES ✳ **COOK TIME 1 HOUR 15 MINUTES** ✳ **MAKES A 20CM CAKE**

Preheat the oven to 160°C/140°C fan/gas mark 3. Grease and line a 18cm round, loose-bottomed cake tin.

Tip the chickpeas into a food processor and blend to a coarse paste. Add the eggs, one at a time, until you have a smooth consistency. Add the almond essence. Transfer the mixture to a mixing bowl and stir through the self-raising flour, baking powder and sugar and beat together. Add the apples and gently mix until they are evenly distributed throughout the mixture. It is quite nice to have a few apples poking through the mixture.

Scrape the cake mixture into the prepared tin. Sprinkle over the flaked almonds and demerara sugar. Bake on the middle shelf of the overn for 45 minutes. Test to see if the centre of the cake is firm to the touch and if you are unsure, return it to the oven for a further 15 minutes. Allow to cool slightly before turning out of the tin onto a wire rack.

Brush the cooled cake with the apricot jam to give it a real 'French patisserie' appearance. Serve warm, in slices.

red

RED SPLIT LENTILS

✳

ADUKI BEANS

✳

KIDNEY BEANS

sweet potato
& red lentil croquettes

INGREDIENTS
1 tablespoon olive oil
1 small onion, finely
  chopped
2 garlic cloves, crushed
125g red split lentils
450g sweet potato, peeled
  and cut into 1cm dice
50g porridge oats
25g mild Cheddar
1 tablespoon roughly
  chopped coriander leaves

FOR THE COATING
75g plain flour
2 medium free-range eggs,
  beaten
100g dried breadcrumbs
2 tablespoons olive oil

These are too fun not to make. My little boys will eat them and that, as any parent knows, is the equivalent to punching the air in an exaggerated high five with internal whooping. The key is to keep the croquettes quite dry and the addition of porridge oats means they are far easier to shape. Just think of the vitamins your kids are unknowingly eating.

PREP TIME 45 MINUTES + 30 MINUTES COOLING ✳ **COOK TIME 1 HOUR** ✳ **MAKES 12**

Heat the oil in a small frying pan. Add the onion and garlic and sauté over a medium heat for 2–3 minutes until just softened. Transfer the mixture to a medium saucepan. Stir the red lentils through the pan, together with the sweet potato and continue to cook for a further 3 minutes. Pour hot water over the lentil and sweet potato mixture until the liquid reaches just 1cm above the level of the mixture. Reduce the heat to low and gently simmer, stirring regularly for 30–40 minutes until everything is soft. Increase the heat for the final few minutes to remove as much liquid as possible. You want a really dry-looking mixture (this makes the croquettes far easier to shape). Remove the frying pan from the heat, tip the contents into a large bowl, mash well and allow to cool completely.

Add the porridge oats, cheese and coriander to the mixture and combine with a firm hand. Divide the mixture into 12 small balls and shape each ball into a croquette.

Preheat the oven to 200°C/180°C fan/gas mark 6.

Put the flour, beaten eggs and breadcrumbs in three separate bowls. Gently roll the croquettes in the flour, dip in the beaten egg and coat in breadcrumbs.

Heat the oil in a large frying pan over a medium–high heat. Fry the croquettes for 2–3 minutes in batches, turning regularly, until the breadcrumbs have become crispy. Remove from the pan and place on a baking sheet. Bake for a further 20 minutes in the oven, or until golden and crispy.

*TIP

This recipe is best approached in two parts. I'd tackle the mixture in the morning and then shape the croquettes at tea time, half an hour before the little people start climbing walls.

creamy red lentil chicken

INGREDIENTS

1 tablespoon vegetable oil

12 skinless, boneless, free-range chicken thighs, kept whole

15g unsalted butter

2 large red onions, quartered

3 large garlic cloves, crushed

1 teaspoon soft brown sugar

1 teaspoon dried chilli flakes

4 tablespoons crunchy peanut butter or any other nut butter

1 tablespoon tomato purée

1 tablespoon mild korma paste or 1 teaspoon mild curry powder

150g red split lentils

400ml can coconut milk

½ medium bunch of coriander, roughly chopped

30g salted peanuts, roughly chopped, to garnish

Salt and freshly ground black pepper

There is a certain creaminess to peanut butter that is difficult to replicate and I'll often add it to a savoury soup or stew. The red lentils almost disappear into the stew, thickening it as they break down.

PREP TIME 25 MINUTES ✳ **COOK TIME 45 MINUTES** ✳ **SERVES 6**

Heat the oil in a large heavy-based casserole dish over a medium heat. Add half the chicken and fry for a few minutes, or until an even, dark golden brown, turning occasionally. Set aside in a warm place while you cook the rest of the chicken, then remove and keep warm.

Melt the butter in the same pan over a medium–low heat, add the onions and fry gently for 5–7 minutes, or until beginning to soften and slightly brown, using a wooden spoon to gently break the onions into petals. Add the garlic and cook for 2 minutes. Add the sugar and cook for a further minute. Stir through the chilli flakes and cook for 2 minutes. Add the peanut butter, tomato purée, korma paste and lentils; stir everything together. Tip the coconut milk into the pan then half-fill the empty can with cold water; add this to the pan also. Bring to the boil, then reduce the heat slightly, cover and simmer for 10 minutes.

Return the browned chicken to the pan and cook for a further 15–20 minutes, or until the lentils have softened and are beginning to break up and the chicken is cooked through. Season to taste and stir through the coriander. Serve topped with a generous handful of the peanuts.

fontina cheese & aduki bean quesadillas

FOR THE PICKLE

1 large red onion, thinly
   sliced
80ml white wine vinegar
5 whole black peppercorns
6 whole coriander seeds
½ teaspoon salt

FOR THE FILLING

400g can aduki beans or
   200g dried aduki beans,
   soaked overnight
1 tablespoon olive oil
1 shallot, finely chopped
1 garlic clove, crushed
1 teaspoon smoked paprika
1 teaspoon ground coriander
½ x 400g can good-quality
   chopped tomatoes
1 heaped teaspoon soft
   brown sugar
Small bunch of coriander,
   roughly chopped
4 large, soft tortilla wraps
150g fontina cheese, cubed
1 avocado, halved, peeled
   and thinly sliced
Salt and freshly ground
   black pepper

A speedy recipe with a Mexican touch, which is ideal for sharing. Warm, soft wraps are loaded with a simple smoked bean mixture, soft cheese and fresh coriander before hitting a griddle (or frying pan) until the filling fuses. The quick red onion pickle is a must; it cuts through the molten cheese and pulls this moreish recipe together.

PREP TIME 45 MINUTES ✳ **COOK TIME 20 MINUTES** ✳ **SERVES 4**

Prepare the pickle by putting the onions, vinegar, peppercorns and coriander seeds in a medium bowl. Sprinkle with the salt, mix thoroughly and set aside to marinate for a good 30 minutes, or until needed. Like many pickles, this one tends to improve the longer it is allowed to mature.

Drain the aduki beans into a sieve and rinse under cold running water. Shake off any excess water and set aside.

Warm the oil in a frying pan. Soften the shallot over a gentle heat until beginning to turn a pale gold. Stir through the garlic and continue to sauté for a further minute before adding the spices and frying for 2–3 minutes until they release their aroma. Pour over the tomatoes and sugar. Taste and adjust the seasoning with salt and black pepper. Spoon the beans into the mixture and cook, uncovered for 10–12 minutes, until the excess liquid has been absorbed and you are left with quite a thick, rich filling. Gently stir through half the coriander.

Cut the tortillas in half and spoon the mixture on one side of the halves. Top with the cheese and the remaining coriander, sandwich the other tortilla on top, press down lightly, and cook in a preheated dry, non-stick frying pan or griddle until lightly coloured, turning to cook the other side. Cut into triangles to serve.

Drain the pickled onions. Serve the quesadillas alongside the pickled onion and with slices of creamy avocado.

✳TIP

If you can't get hold of fontina use Gouda or Gruyère cheese; they too melt beautifully.

hippie bowl

INGREDIENTS

150g brown rice, rinsed
½ x 400g can aduki beans,
    drained and rinsed
2 large free-range eggs
70g raw baby spinach leaves,
    sliced
4 spring onions, trimmed
    and chopped
½ red chilli, deseeded and
    finely sliced
½ ripe avocado, halved,
    peeled and sliced
2 tablespoons roasted
    peanuts
Salt and freshly ground
    black pepper

FOR THE VINAIGRETTE

2 tablespoons olive oil
1 teaspoon Dijon mustard
1 tablespoon cider vinegar
Juice of ½ lemon

If health could come in the form of a recipe, this would come close to ticking the right boxes. A protein-packed, filling yet not bloating bowl with brown rice, eggs, avocado and chilli – perfect for days when your body requires a health fix.

PREP TIME 20 MINUTES ✳ COOK TIME 30 MINUTES ✳ SERVES 2

Empty the rice and a pinch of salt into a large saucepan and cover generously with cold water, about twice the volume of the rice. Bring to the boil, cover with a tight-fitting lid and reduce the heat so that the water simmers rather than boils. Cook on a gentle simmer for 25 minutes until the rice is tender and the liquid has almost been soaked up. Drain any remaining liquid and fluff the rice with a fork, returning it to its cooking pan. Stir through the aduki beans to warm through.

Meanwhile, cook the eggs. Bring a saucepan of water to a simmer, rather than a full-blown boil. Carefully add the eggs to the pan and cook for 7 minutes – the whites will be cooked and the yolks should still be very slightly soft. Drain and run cold water over the eggs to stop them cooking further. When cool enough to handle, tap them on the work surface to crack the shells, allowing air to reach the whites, and peel them. Cut the eggs into quarters.

Stir the spinach, half the spring onions and a little of the chilli into the rice.

Make the dressing by whisking all the ingredients together in a small jug. Season to taste with a little salt and black pepper. Set aside for a minute before pouring the dressing over the warm rice and stirring in lightly.

Pile the rice into two deep bowls and top with the remaining chopped spring onions, avocado, remaining chilli, a sprinkling of peanuts and quarters of hard-boiled egg.

✳TIP

To prevent excess browning, squeeze lemon juice over the sliced avocado if you are making the dish in advance.

red cabbage, crispy kale & aduki bean salad

INGREDIENTS
½ small red cabbage
150ml sunflower oil, for
   frying
250g kale, torn into
   5–6cm pieces
400g can aduki beans,
   drained and rinsed
60g hazelnuts, toasted
   and crushed
Salt and freshly ground
   black pepper

FOR THE DRESSING
80ml buttermilk
2 tablespoons mayonnaise
1 teaspoon lemon juice
3 tablespoons finely
   chopped dill fronds

This is a stunning, substantial autumnal number for the months when green isn't quite in vogue. You could go down the slower, more considered, route of simmering dried beans in stock and herbs until soft, but I opted for a can of beans, rinsed and warmed through with butter. Toast the hazelnuts as it deepens the flavour and brings the salad together.

PREP TIME 15 MINUTES ✳ COOK TIME 10 MINUTES ✳ SERVES 4

Cut out the core of the cabbage and, using a mandolin or sharp knife, shred the cabbage as finely as your knife skills will allow. Set aside.

Heat the oil in a large heavy-based saucepan over a medium heat until hot, just below smoking point. Add the kale in several batches – be sure to wear an apron, the kale will hiss and spit as it hits the oil. Fry each batch for 3–5 minutes, or until curling up and crispy. Transfer to a plate lined with kitchen paper and scrunch over a little salt. Leave to cool.

To make the dressing, whisk together the buttermilk, mayonnaise and lemon juice in a small bowl. Stir through the dill and season to taste, adding a touch more lemon juice if needed.

Tip the cabbage and beans into a huge bowl and stir through half the toasted hazelnuts. Decant onto a large platter and top with the crispy kale and remaining nuts. Drizzle over the dressing and serve.

baked lamb meatballs with kidney bean tomato sauce

FOR THE MEATBALLS
500g lamb mince
3 anchovy fillets, chopped
40g fresh breadcrumbs
Zest of 1 unwaxed lemon
2 garlic cloves, crushed
3 tablespoons chopped
    basil leaves
3 tablespoons vegetable oil
Salt and freshly ground
    black pepper

FOR THE SAUCE
1 tablespoon vegetable oil
2 onions, finely sliced
2 garlic cloves, sliced
1 teaspoon ground cumin
2 tablespoons tomato purée
2 x 400g cans chopped
    tomatoes
400g can kidney beans,
    drained and rinsed
1 tablespoon balsamic
    vinegar
2 tablespoons chopped
    flat-leaf parsley
125g ball mozzarella cheese
Basil leaves, to garnish

The humble meatball is undergoing rehab and we watch as this reliable recipe has moved from school canteen to stylish restaurant. This version, made with minced lamb, salted anchovy, lemon and basil is cooked atop a thick beany, sauce and served just as, no pasta needed. Dreamy family food.

PREP TIME 20 MINUTES ✳ **COOK TIME 50 MINUTES** ✳ **SERVES 4**

Start by making the meatballs. Put the lamb mince, anchovies, breadcrumbs, lemon zest, half the garlic and the basil in a large bowl. Use your hands to mix everything together really thoroughly. Season well, then shape into 12 balls, roughly the size of a golf ball.

Heat the oil in a deep, heavy-based frying pan over a medium heat. Add the meatballs, in batches, and cook for a good 5–6 minutes, occasionally turning with tongs, until really brown all over. Try not to move them too much during frying or you risk them falling apart. Remove from the pan and set aside while you make the sauce. Preheat the oven to 180°C/160°C fan/gas mark 4.

To make the sauce, wipe out the frying pan and heat the oil over a fairly high heat and add the onions. Let them colour slightly before adding the garlic and cumin. Stir as they cook for a couple of minutes, before adding the tomato purée. Increase the heat and add the tomatoes. Cook for 20 minutes or so until the sauce has thickened. Remove from the heat and stir through the kidney beans, vinegar and parsley.

Tip the sauce into a 2-litre ovenproof dish and nestle the meatballs in it. Top with roughly torn mozzarella and crack over some black pepper. Cook for 25 minutes. Remove from the oven and serve, garnished with fresh basil.

cheese, chutney
& kidney bean burgers

INGREDIENTS

2 x 400g cans kidney beans,
   drained and rinsed
2 tablespoons chutney
1 medium egg, beaten
1 teaspoon wholegrain
   mustard
1 teaspoon brown sugar
3 tablespoons roughly
   chopped flat-leaf parsley
100g rolled porridge oats
75g Cheddar, finely grated
Salt and freshly ground
   black pepper

FOR THE COATING

75g plain flour
2 medium free-range eggs,
   beaten
100g dried breadcrumbs
2 tablespoons vegetable oil

TO SERVE

Avocado, peeled and sliced
Gherkins, sliced
Mayonnaise
Dill fronds

It is known all too well that veggie burgers can be a dire thing – dry, tasteless, with no body to hold them together. Well, these patties compete with their meaty friends in the flavour stakes, with a little grated cheese and chutney run through the mixture to add both flavour and body. Top with all the trimmings – avocado, gherkins and mayo to finish off the burger.

PREP TIME 15 MINUTES + 30 MINUTES CHILLING ✳ **COOK TIME 30 MINUTES** ✳ **SERVES 6**

Tip the kidney beans into the bowl of a food processor with the chutney, beaten egg, mustard and sugar. Process to form a soft mixture. Tip into a bowl and stir through the parsley, oats and cheese. Season with salt and black pepper. Leave the mixture to chill for 30 minutes in the fridge to soak up moisture and allow the flavours to develop.

The chilled burger mixture should be thick and pliable. Shape into 6 thick patties about the size of a digestive biscuit. Put the flour, beaten eggs and breadcrumbs in three separate bowls. Gently coat the patties in the flour, dip in the beaten egg and coat in breadcrumbs.

Heat the oil in a large frying pan over a medium heat. Fry the burgers for 8–10 minutes each side, until the breadcrumbs have become crispy. They should be golden, crispy and hot all the way through.

Serve the burgers alongside the avocado, gherkins, a touch of mayonnaise and garnish with some dill.

chilli con carne

INGREDIENTS

1 tablespoon olive oil
1 red onion, chopped
½ tablespoon soft brown
  sugar
3 garlic cloves, crushed
3 teaspoons ground cumin
2 teaspoons ground
  coriander
1½ teaspoons hot chilli
  flakes
½ teaspoon ground
  cinnamon
1 teaspoon smoked paprika
½ nutmeg, grated
500g beef mince
200g tube tomato purée
300ml red wine
200ml hot beef stock
400g can chopped tomatoes
2 x 400g cans red kidney
  beans, drained and rinsed
50g dark chocolate, broken
  into pieces
½ bunch of fresh coriander,
  roughly chopped
Juice of ½ lime
Salt and freshly ground
  black pepper

This is a wonderful recipe for a family dinner. Children will be intrigued by the addition of chocolate, just as the chilli is taken off the heat. Adjust the amount of chilli according to your family's tolerance.

PREP TIME 15 MINUTES ✳ **COOK TIME 55 MINUTES** ✳ **SERVES 8**

Heat the oil in a large casserole dish over a medium heat. Add the onion and fry for 5 minutes until beginning to soften and turn slightly golden. Stir through the sugar and sauté for a further 2 minutes before adding the garlic and spices, then cook for a final minute.

Increase the heat and tip in the mince, breaking it up well with a wooden spoon. Leave it to colour without stirring for a good 3–4 minutes, then, as the meat on the bottom is starting to brown, stir again, breaking up the meat where necessary and leave to colour. Once the beef is brown, stir though the tomato purée. Add the wine, reduce the heat and simmer until reduced by half.

Pour over the beef stock and tomatoes and increase the heat to a boil. Stir through the kidney beans. Cover with a lid, reduce the heat until there are barely any bubbles and cook gently for 45 minutes.

Finally, stir through the chocolate until melted and combined. Season to taste and top with the coriander and a generous squeeze of lime. Serve with steamed rice.

rye, chocolate
& aduki bean cookies

INGREDIENTS

200g unsalted butter,
  softened
200g light brown sugar
125g caster sugar
400g can aduki beans,
  drained and rinsed
1 large egg
1 teaspoon vanilla extract
325g rye or white flour
¾ teaspoon bicarbonate
  of soda
1 teaspoon baking powder
1 teaspoon sea salt
300g chocolate (a mixture
  of white, dark and milk,
  chopped into chunks)

A freshly baked biscuit can be used as many kinds of currency from straightforward bribery to less obvious peace-keeping. This mixture can be kept sealed in the fridge for any such moments and you'll be eating cookies 15 minutes later. The beans make for a chewy, soft texture and are a very suitable partner for the generous amount of chocolate. Use rye or white flour – both work well and it should come down to preference.

PREP TIME 15 MINUTES + 2 HOURS CHILLING ✳ COOK TIME 15 MINUTES ✳ MAKES 16

Beat the butter and sugars together for 2 minutes, until pale and fluffy in consistency. Add the aduki beans and continue to whisk until the beans have blended in, but their purple skins are still visible in the mixture. Add the egg and vanilla extract.

Sift together the flour, bicarbonate of soda and baking powder. Add the salt. Stir the dry ingredients into the wet mixture to form a sticky dough. Stir through the mountain of chocolate. Cover and chill the mixture for at least 2 hours but preferably two to three days for the flavours to deepen.

When ready to bake, preheat the oven to 180°C/160°C fan/gas mark 4. Line two or three trays with baking parchment and use an ice-cream scoop or a large spoon to form 16 balls of cookie dough. Space the balls out well as they will spread – five to six per tray is about right. Bake for 15 minutes until pale golden. Remove from the oven and leave on the tray to firm up before transferring to a wire rack to cool while you cook the next batch.

hot chocolate bean & almond cake

INGREDIENTS

400g can kidney beans,
  drained and rinsed
250g unsalted butter,
  softened, plus extra to
  grease
225g light brown sugar
3 medium free-range eggs
2 teaspoons vanilla essence
100g good-quality dark
  chocolate, melted
200g ground almonds
1 teaspoon bicarbonate
  of soda
25g cocoa powder
75ml boiling water

FOR THE ICING

170g salted butter, softened
350g icing sugar
2–3 tablespoons milk

TO DECORATE

Coconut flakes, toasted
Raspberries

This cake has a wicked mousse-like texture. The almonds and beans negate the need for flour, and so this cake is also a treat suitable for any friends who need or like to avoid gluten.

PREP TIME 30 MINUTES ✳ **COOK TIME 45 MINUTES** ✳ **SERVES 8**

Preheat the oven to 200°C/180°C fan/gas mark 6. Grease and line two 20cm loose-bottomed cake tins.

Tip the kidney beans into a bowl and use a hand-held blender, or the smaller compartment of a food processor, to blend them to a thick paste, adding a drop of water if needed. Set aside.

Put the butter and sugar into a large mixing bowl and beat using an electric mixer for a few minutes until the mixture is pale and fluffy. Add the eggs, one at a time, beating well after each addition. Gradually add the vanilla essence and melted chocolate, beating well. Beat in the kidney bean paste and ground almonds. Switch to a large spoon and stir through the bicarbonate of soda and cocoa powder. Pour in the boiling water and beat well.

Carefully pour the batter into the prepared tins and bake for 30 minutes. Reduce the heat to 170°C/150°C fan/gas mark 3 and bake for a further 30 minutes, or until a skewer inserted into the centre comes out almost clean. Don't worry if it's a bit sticky – the cake will continue to cook as it cools. Remove from the oven and leave to cool in the tin for 30 minutes, then transfer to a wire rack.

To make the icing, beat the butter until soft and pale using an electric beater, then add the sugar and beat until smooth and creamy, adding enough milk to achieve a good consistency.

Once the cakes are cool, turn one upside down on a plate or board, spread it with a good third of the icing, then sandwich with the second cake. Spread the remaining buttercream on top and decorate with toasted coconut flakes and fresh raspberries.

brown

SPLIT FAVA BEANS

✳

BORLOTTI BEANS

✳

PINTO BEANS

fennel & fava bean soup with rosemary rye bread

INGREDIENTS

175g dried split fava beans, soaked overnight and drained
2 tablespoons olive oil
1 onion, diced
2 celery sticks, diced
4 large garlic cloves, diced
4 bay leaves
2 teaspoons fennel seeds
2 litres hot vegetable stock
50g pumpkin seeds
Salt and freshly ground black pepper

FOR THE PARMESAN RYE BREAD

400g rye flour, plus extra for dusting
100g strong white bread flour
Pinch of salt
10g instant yeast
1 tablespoon black treacle
Olive oil, for kneading

A soup with peasant origins, made thick with fava beans. The aniseed flavour of the fennel seeds (a must for any home storecupboard) really gives the soup character. Eat in the deepest depths of winter with warm rye bread and lashings of butter.

PREP TIME 30 MINUTES + OVERNIGHT SOAKING
✳ **COOK TIME 2 HOURS 15 MINUTES** ✳ **SERVES 8**

For the bread, tip the flours into a large mixing bowl. Add the salt, yeast, treacle and 275ml cold water and mix together until it's incorporated. You may need to add a touch more water – the aim is for a soft, pliable dough. Tip the dough onto a clean, oiled work surface and knead for 5–10 minutes until the dough comes together. Form into a smooth loaf shape and place on a floured baking sheet. Cover with a tea towel and allow to prove for an afternoon or at least 6 hours. Knock back the dough, kneading it for a further 2–3 minutes before shaping it into a small loaf and leaving it to rise for 30 minutes.

Preheat the oven to 220°C/200°C fan/gas mark 7. Place a baking sheet in the oven to heat up. Make four or five horizontal cuts across the loaf, each just breaking the surface. Bake for 30 minutes or until the base sounds just hollow. Once cooked, make 6–8 more deep cuts into the loaf (but don't slice all the way through). Push stems of rosemary into the slices, drizzle with 1 tablespoon olive oil and return to the oven for 5 minutes.

Meanwhile, drain the soaked beans and rinse under cold, running water and set aside.

Heat the oil in a large casserole over a medium heat. Add the onion, celery and garlic and gently fry for 6–8 minutes until the vegetables have softened and turned translucent. Add the bay leaves and fennel seeds and continue to cook for a further minute. Stir through the beans and pour over the stock. Simmer for 2 hours until the beans are perfectly tender. Remove the bay leaves and blend in batches and return to the saucepan to heat through. Season to taste.

Tip the pumpkin seeds into a dry frying pan over a high heat and toast the seeds until their skins buckle. Serve the soup in lovely big bowls, topped with black pepper and the toasted pumpkin seeds.

fava bean & tomato loaf with herb yogurt

FOR THE LOAF

450g dried split fava beans
1 medium onion, halved
1 bay leaf
220g tomato purée
4 medium eggs, lightly
  beaten
200g porridge oats
2 teaspoons capers,
  roughly chopped
8–10 small gherkins,
  roughly chopped
120g sun-dried tomatoes,
  roughly chopped
½ small bunch of flat-leaf
  parsley, finely chopped

FOR THE TOPPING

15g butter
30g porridge oats
40g hazelnuts, toasted
  and crushed

FOR THE YOGURT

150ml Greek yogurt
Small bunch of basil, finely
  chopped
1 small garlic clove, grated
A little fresh lemon juice
Salt and freshly ground
  black pepper, to taste

Hodmeadod's is an outstanding British company that is putting pulses back on the map. The beans, sourced from all over England, herald forgotten varieties such as the black badger bean and split fava, making them feel contemporary and enticing. This loaf is a variation on their loaf served at Pulse Feast – part of a global celebration to mark the launch of the International Year of the Pulses in 2015.

PREP TIME 40 MINUTES ✳ **COOK TIME 50 MINUTES** ✳ **MAKES 1 X 900G LOAF**

Soak the beans overnight in plenty of cold water. Rinse the beans, tip them in a heavy-based saucepan and place on a moderate heat. Cover with cold water, add the onion and bay leaf and bring to the boil. Reduce the temperature slightly and simmer for 20–30 minutes until the beans are tender but not falling apart. Fish out the onion and bay leaf and discard. Drain the beans and decant into a large mixing bowl.

Preheat the oven to 180°C/160°C fan/ gas mark 6.

For the topping, melt the butter in a frying pan over a moderate heat. Stir through the oats and hazelnuts and toast lightly for 2–3 minutes.

Return to the loaf preparation: add the tomato purée, eggs, oats, capers, gherkins, sun-dried tomatoes and parsley to the cooked beans and combine well. Transfer to a non-stick 900g loaf tin. Top with the nuts and bake for 40–50 minutes, or until firm and piping hot in the centre. Remove the loaf from the oven and allow to cool in the tin for a good 10 minutes before turning out.

Meanwhile, make the yogurt. In a small bowl, combine the yogurt, basil and garlic. Season to taste with lemon juice, salt and a good grind of black pepper.

Serve warm, thick slices of the loaf with a dollop of the basil yogurt and a peppery rocket salad.

crispy miso fava beans

INGREDIENTS

150g dried split fava beans
2 tablespoons olive oil
2 teaspoons miso paste
2–3 tablespoons Parmesan,
  finely grated
Salt and freshly ground
  black pepper

Quick to pull together and requiring minimum effort, this party nibble is so moreish. Serve warm from the oven, just as they are, or add to a salad for crunch.

PREP TIME 5 MINUTES ✳ COOK TIME 1 HOUR 10 MINUTES ✳ ENOUGH FOR 8 TO NIBBLE ON

Bring a large saucepan of salted water to the boil. Add the beans and simmer for 25–30 minutes until tender but not losing their shape. The timing will largely depend on the age and size of the beans – don't be afraid to give them an extra few minutes.

Meanwhile, preheat the oven to 200°C/180°C fan/gas mark 6.

Drain the beans, return them to the saucepan and season well. Mix the oil with the miso paste. Delicately combine this with the beans, dressing them in seasoned miso oil. Spread out the beans on a large baking sheet, ensuring they are in a single layer and bake for 25 minutes. Remove the sheet from the oven and spoon through the Parmesan. Gently combine and return the beans to the oven for a further 15 minutes. Allow to cool slightly before serving in bowls.

tuscan borlotti bean, kale & tomato lasagne

INGREDIENTS

2 tablespoons olive oil
2 onions, roughly chopped
A few thyme sprigs,
    leaves picked
3 large garlic cloves, crushed
4 tablespoons tomato purée
2 x 400g cans good-quality
    chopped tomatoes
400g can borlotti beans,
    drained and rinsed
A small knob of butter
200g kale, washed and
    roughly chopped
1–1½ teaspoons freshly
    grated nutmeg
400ml crème fraîche
250g fresh lasagne sheets
60g Parmesan, finely grated
Salt and freshly ground
    black pepper
Fresh basil, to garnish

Green is my favourite colour, 26 my lucky number and lasagna my favourite meal. This is a striking version of the Italian masterpiece, layered with crème fraîche, borlotti and blanched kale, but shortcuts have been made to make it suitable for the modern cook. Crème fraîche makes for the sauce (note, not half fat) and the filling needs little cooking. Layering is difficult to specify but, as a rule of thumb, be sure to start and finish with a layer of sauce.

PREP TIME 25 MINUTES ✳ COOK TIME 1 HOUR ✳ SERVES 8

Preheat the oven to 180°C/160°C fan/gas mark 4.

Heat the oil in a large, deep saucepan over a medium heat. Add the onions and cook fairly gently for 8–10 minutes until they have softened and turned the colour of bronze. Add the thyme leaves to the pan with the garlic and cook for a further minute. Stir through the tomato purée. Tip in the tomatoes, reduce the temperature and gently cook, uncovered, for 25–30 minutes, or until the sauce reduces by half. Season and stir the borlotti beans into the tomato sauce.

Meanwhile, melt the butter in a large saucepan over a medium heat. Throw in the kale and season liberally with nutmeg, salt and black pepper. Cook, covered, for 4–5 minutes until the kale softens and wilts.

Spread a few spoonfuls – about one-third – of the crème fraîche over the base of a deep 2-litre ovenproof dish. Cover with a single layer of fresh pasta. Spoon over half the tomato bolotti mixture, half the kale and a sprinkling of Parmesan. Cover with fresh pasta followed by a second layer of crème fraîche followed by the remaining tomato sauce, then kale. Finish with a final layer of lasagne sheets and the remaining crème fraîche. Sprinkle with Parmesan and a little more black pepper.

Transfer to the middle shelf of the oven and cook for 35–40 minutes, or until the top has nicely browned. Remove from the oven and leave to stand for 5 minutes. The pasta sheets will soak up all the liquid, making it easier to cut in portions. Serve in squares, garnished with basil.

slow-cooked ox cheeks with parmesan polenta

INGREDIENTS
250g dried borlotti beans, soaked overnight and drained
2 tablespoons olive oil
3 shallots, chopped
3 garlic cloves, crushed
1 teaspoon ras el hanout
½ teaspoon ground cumin
½ teaspoon ground coriander
1 small preserved lemon, sliced
1 tablespoon tomato purée
160ml red wine
1 litre hot beef stock
4 ox cheeks (about 1.5kg)
3 tablespoons chopped flat-leaf parsley
Salt and freshly ground black pepper
Zest of 1 unwaxed lemon

FOR THE POLENTA
1 litre hot vegetable stock
200g polenta
100ml single cream
50g butter
50g Parmesan, finely grated

Ox cheeks are a satisfying piece of meat, predictably full bodied with a lean, muscular texture. Like the dried borlotti, they require long and slow cooking, and this recipe allows both ingredients hours to absorb flavour and develop a soft, gentle texture. Preserved lemon serves to intensify the story of this stew.

PREP TIME 30 MINUTES + OVERNIGHT SOAKING
✳ **COOK TIME 4 HOURS 30 MINUTES** ✳ **SERVES 4**

Bring a large saucepan of salted water to the boil. Add the beans and simmer for 20 minutes, just to take the edge off them; they will have a longer, slower cook in the stew. Drain and set aside.

Heat the oil in a large casserole dish over a medium heat and fry the shallots gently for 4–6 minutes until softened. Add the garlic and cook for a further 3 minutes. Add the spices to the casserole and cook for a further minute. Stir though the preserved lemon and tomato purée. Pour in the wine and cook until the liquid is reduced by half.

Add the stock, beans and ox cheeks to the casserole and bring to the boil. Reduce the heat, cover with a tight-fitting lid and cook for 4 hours, or until the meat is tender and falling apart. Check the dish every hour or so to make sure it isn't drying out – top up with a little water if it needs it. Season to taste.

Twenty minutes before you are ready to serve, start on the polenta. Bring the vegetable stock to the boil in a medium saucepan. Slowly tip in the polenta and stir as quickly as your wrists allow. Bubble the polenta for a few minutes, stirring, until thickened. Remove the pan from the heat, stir in the butter and Parmesan. Season really well – I like mine peppery.

Stir 2 tablespoons of the parsley through the casserole. Spoon the polenta onto four warmed plates and top each with stew, the remaining parsley and the lemon zest. Serve.

autumn veg minestrone with parsley & walnut pesto

INGREDIENTS

2 tablespoons olive oil

1 small red onion, finely
  chopped

3 carrots, cut into small
  cubes

½ small squash (about
  300g), peeled and cut
  into small cubes

3–4 celery sticks and
  any leaves

3 rosemary sprigs, finely
  chopped

2 garlic cloves, crushed

200ml red wine

400g can chopped tomatoes

1.25 litres hot vegetable
  stock

400g can pinto beans,
  drained and rinsed

500g rainbow chard or
  cavolo nero, stalks
  removed and leaves very
  roughly chopped

Salt and freshly ground
  black pepper

FOR THE PESTO

3 large handfuls of flat-leaf
  parsley (about 30g)

1 garlic clove, crushed

60g walnuts, lightly toasted

150ml olive oil, plus extra
  to drizzle

30g Parmesan, finely grated

Minestrone is an Italian masterpiece that has been refined by generations of grandmothers handing scribbled notes to their children. The result is a wonderfully healthy bowl of soup, which is expertly complemented by a carafe of Italian wine. See page 161 for recipe photograph.

PREP TIME 25 MINUTES ✳ COOK TIME 1 HOUR 10 MINUTES ✳ SERVES 8

Heat the oil in a deep saucepan over a low-medium heat. Add the onion, carrots, squash, celery and rosemary to the pan and gently sweat for 10 minutes until the onion and celery have softened. You aren't looking to colour the vegetables, so reduce the heat slightly if needed. Add the garlic and cook for a further 1–2 minutes. Pour over the wine and simmer until the liquid has reduced by half.

Add the tomatoes and stock to the pan and bring to the boil. Reduce the heat to a simmer, cover with a lid but set it askew to allow some of the steam to escape. Cook gently for 45 minutes, stirring occasionally. Finally, add the beans and chard and cook for a further 10 minutes. Season to taste.

Meanwhile, make the pesto. Put the parsley, garlic and walnuts into the bowl of a food processer and whizz to a paste. Transfer to a bowl and stir through the oil and Parmesan. Season to taste.

Taste the soup for seasoning. Pour into bowls and drizzle with the pesto and a touch of extra oil if you like.

borlotti, courgette, asparagus & olive salad

INGREDIENTS

225g fresh borlotti beans
2 courgettes, cut into ½ cm
 slices on the diagonal
1–2 tablespoons olive oil
100g asparagus tips
Handful of basil leaves
Zest of 1 unwaxed lemon
75g black olives, pitted

FOR THE DRESSING

3 tablespoons olive oil
Juice of 1 lemon
Pinch of caster sugar
½ garlic clove, crushed

Asparagus and courgette herald the beginning of spring. Combined with fresh borlotti, this salad is a lovely partnership with a nod towards Italy. Double the dressing if you're like me and enjoy mopping it up with bread.

PREP TIME 15 MINUTES ✳ COOK TIME 25 MINUTES ✳ SERVES 4

Tip the beans into a small saucepan of simmering water. Cook for 25-30 minutes until their colour has faded somewhat and the beans are tender. Set aside to cool slightly.

Meanwhile, put a griddle pan over a high heat. Brush the courgette slices with the oil and place them on the hot griddle. Be careful not to overlap the slices – you want them to fry rather than steam. Leave them to cook, undisturbed, until you have recogniseable griddle lines. Turn over and repeat. Remove from the pan and set aside while you do the same for the remaining slices and the asparagus tips.

Make the dressing by combining all the ingredients in a mug or jam jar. Stir until all has amalgamated. Taste and stir through a little more lemon juice, if you wish.

In a large bowl, toss together the cooled beans, griddled courgettes, asparagus, most of the basil leaves (keeping a few back for garnish), lemon zest and black olives. Dress the salad and decant onto a generous platter, garnished with the remaining basil leaves.

clams with borlotti beans & tarragon

INGREDIENTS

2 tablespoons olive oil

3 shallots, finely chopped

4 garlic cloves, finely sliced

Small handful of flat-leaf parsley

Pinch of dried chilli flakes

150ml white wine

400g can borlotti beans, drained

1kg clams, cleaned (ensure they are really clean: scrub the shells, tug off the beards and discard any that refuse to close or are broken)

1 lemon, sliced

300ml hot vegetable stock

Small handful of tarragon and flat-leaf parsley, leaves finely chopped

Salt and freshly ground black pepper

A clean, honest, Venetian classic that really doesn't need an introduction. Quick to put together and as virtuous a caldron of food as one might hope for. I quite enjoy the theatre of presenting the clams in their shells, but the cook could easily pinch the flesh from their shells and return them to the hot broth pre-table.

PREP TIME 20 MINUTES + OVERNIGHT SOAKING ✳ **COOK TIME 20 MINUTES** ✳ **SERVES 4**

Pour a generous glug of oil into a heavy-based casserole dish. Add the shallots, garlic and a good pinch of salt and black pepper.

Tear the stalks from the parsley leaves, roughly chop the stalks and add to the casserole. Crumble in the chilli and cook over a moderate heat for about 4 minutes until fragrant and the shallots are tinged with gold.

Turn up the heat to high, pour in the wine and cook until almost evaporated before tipping in the beans, clams, lemon and stock. The casserole will be filled with fury and steam, so give everything a good shake and cover with the lid. After about 4 minutes, the clam shells will tentatively start to open. Keep shaking the pan until all of them have opened, discarding any that have remained closed. Stir in the tarragon and parsley leaves and serve in warmed bowls with fresh bread for mopping up the juices.

proscuitto-wrapped pork with tomato & herb borlotti

INGREDIENTS

200g dried borlotti beans, soaked overnight and drained

300–400g pork tenderloin fillet

5–6 slices of Parma ham (prosciutto)

1 tablespoon olive oil

3 shallots, finely sliced

4 garlic cloves, crushed

1 teaspoon sugar

2 x 400g cans good-quality chopped tomatoes

1 tablespoon red wine vinegar

Small bunch of basil, chopped

Handful of flat-leaf parsley, chopped

Salt and freshly ground black pepper

Pork tenderloin is an underused ingredient in my opinion. Far more reasonably priced than you might expect and as lean and soft as you could want for. Wrapped in prosciutto, seared and served atop thick, intense sweet beans, this is a meal waiting to be cooked. If you didn't want to use pork, chicken would work well too.

PREP TIME 1 HOUR 30 MINUTES + OVERNIGHT SOAKING ✳ **COOK TIME 1 HOUR** ✳ **SERVES 4**

Put the beans into a large saucepan and cover with twice their volume of cold water. Bring the pan to a quick boil over a medium heat, then reduce the temperature, cover the pan and simmer for 1–1½ hours, until the beans are tender. This time will depend on how old/fresh the beans are, so keep a fairly watchful eye. Drain and set aside.

Preheat the oven to 180°C/160°C fan/gas mark 4.

Season the pork fillet and lay the strips of Parma ham on the worktop, slightly overlapping. Place the fillet on top and use the slices to wrap it up. Tie the fillet with cook's string at roughly 5cm intervals to hold the whole thing together.

Heat the oil in a heavy-based frying pan over a medium heat and, using tongs, sear the pork until beautifully golden on all sides. Remove the pork from the pan and set aside to rest.

Add a drop more oil to the dish if needed and add the shallots. Fry for a few minutes until translucent, then stir through the garlic and sugar and cook for a further minute. Add the beans, tomatoes and vinegar and give everything a good muddle, season well and simmer for 30–40 minutes until the sauce has thickened and reduced slightly. Remove from the heat and stir through most of the herbs (reserve some for serving). Tip into a suitable ovenproof dish.

Place the seared pork fillet on top of the beans, cutting it in half if needed, and put in the oven for 20 minutes until the pork is cooked through. Remove from the oven and allow the dish to rest for 5–7 minutes. Slice the pork and serve with the beans, generously sprinkled with the remaining herbs.

pecan & borlotti cakes with brown sugar icing

INGREDIENTS

400g can borlotti beans, drained and rinsed
125g pecans
120g gluten-free plain flour
1 teaspoon baking powder (gluten-free if required)
125g soft, dark brown sugar
3 medium eggs
Pinch of salt
1 teaspoon vanilla extract

FOR THE BROWN SUGAR ICING

110g salted butter
220g soft dark brown sugar
Pinch of salt
60ml milk, plus a little extra
350g icing sugar, sifted
12 whole pecans, to garnish

These gluten-free throw-it-all-into-the-mixer cakes produce a deep, caramelised, dark brown sugar hit. As with all cake baking made with beans, the cakes have a moreish density to them that I love. The icing is stunning and one to use again and again. I imagine it would sit well atop a chocolate cake.

PREP TIME 40 MINUTES ✳ **COOK TIME 20 MINUTES** ✳ **MAKES 12 CUPCAKES**

Preheat the oven to 180°C/160°C fan/gas mark 4. Line a 12-hole cupcake tray with paper cases.

This is more or less an all-in-one method, so have everything ready. Put the beans and pecans into the bowl of a food processor and pulse until you have a coarse paste. Add the flour, baking powder and sugar and process until combined. Crack the eggs into the mixture, one at a time, with the motor still running. Finally, add the salt and vanilla extract. Divide the mixture between the cupcake cases and bake for 20 minutes, or until the centre of the cakes springs back when touched. Remove from the oven and allow to cool.

For the icing, melt the butter in a saucepan and stir in the sugar and the salt. Bring to the boil and boil for 2–3 minutes, stirring constantly. Stir through the milk and return the pan to the boil for a second time. Remove from the heat and allow to cool until the mixture is lukewarm – this will take at least 15 minutes. Stir in the sifted icing sugar and beat with a wooden spoon until smooth. Add a tiny bit of milk, if needed, to achieve a soft consistency. Pipe generously onto the cupcakes and serve, garnished with a pecan.

index

thank you

Never having given a speech on my wedding day - and always slightly regretting it – I feel this is an outlet to say a very public thank you to a few of my special people.

Kyle Books have generously walked with me for six years now, commissioning new recipes, encouraging new ideas and allowing me to run with innovative ingredients. Sophie, my constant editor throughout the years, is the nicest person you would hope to meet and doing the photography with her beautiful sister, Ali, was a double treat. The shoot location being in sunny Brighton, just a mile or two from home, made for the dreamiest of days.

My assistants Esther, Lola and Sophie have sparked ideas, generously tested recipes and helped me through this journey of beans and pulses. Thank you.

My growing family. Each book I have published has fallen in sync with the arrival of a new baby. Jasper and Wilberforce, 4 and 2 years old have eaten their fair share of chickpeas and become strangely used to baked beans not being spooned from a tin. My new baby, who will have been born by the time this is published, allowed me just enough energy to enjoy the shoots and thankfully, allowed me to test recipes both day and night without (the dreaded) morning sickness. Thank you for that. And Nick, my husband who has, as the expression goes, given me wings. I love you.